ONE POT

FROM THE KITCHENS OF
Martha Stewart Living

ONE POT

120+ easy meals from your skillet, slow cooker, stockpot, and more

Photographs by Christina Holmes and others

CLARKSON POTTER/PUBLISHERS
NEW YORK

CLARKSON POTTER is a trademark
and POTTER with colophon is a registered
trademark of Random House LLC.

Library of Congress
Cataloging-in-Publication Data
is available.

ISBN 978-0-307-95441-1
eBook ISBN 978-0-307-95442-8

Printed in China

Cover and book design by Gillian MacLeod
Cover photographs by Christina Holmes
See page 247 for a complete list of photo credits.

10 9 8 7 6 5 4 3 2 1

First Edition

This book is dedicated to everyone who is searching, searching, searching for easy and nutritious meals to feed the family.

Contents

Introduction

This book comes at an opportune time. We are all so busy, with a myriad of obligations that distract us from the kitchen and electronic devices that lure us from the stove. Here is an excellent solution: the *One Pot* solution. With this collection of recipes, we can all get delicious, healthy, easy meals on the table on a daily basis. This practical approach to cooking makes preparation much simpler—and cleanup much quicker.

Our one-pot dishes are cleverly designed to combine varied tastes and textures using interesting but accessible ingredients. The recipes make use of six different types of cookware—and the results clearly demonstrate the distinctive features of each. The Dutch oven cooks slowly and renders tender results. The skillet is ideal for sautéing, the stockpot for simmering. The roasting pan can be used for more than roasts—add other ingredients, and everything cooks perfectly in one delightful dish (see Lamb with Asparagus and Potatoes, opposite). The slow cooker permits us to put a meal together in minutes and let it cook on its own for hours. The old-fashioned pressure cooker has become the new darling of the kitchen, speeding up long preparations while preserving taste, color, and flavor in amazing ways. (And the new versions are well priced and do not terrify us as much as the "vintage" models!)

You probably already have the necessary cookware in your kitchen. I hope this book helps you use all of it to create masterpieces for yourself, your friends, and your family, each and every day.

Martha Stewart

P.S. Of course, we didn't forget dessert. In the spirit of our streamlined dinners that don't require much of our time or effort, we've included ten of our favorite finales: cakes, cookies, rustic fruit desserts, and more—each one as easy as the next.

Dutch Oven

The Dutch oven is ideal for the quintessential one-pot meal: a long-simmered stew or braise with fork-tender meat and vegetables. The hefty, good-looking pot goes from the stovetop to the oven and even to the center of the dinner table.

The Basics

A Dutch oven is a heavy pot, usually cast iron, with a lid. It also goes by the name French oven (the pot called a braiser is similar, but tends to be a little shallower). Whatever you call it, this vessel excels at stewing and braising: browning ingredients and then adding liquid. (The main difference between stewing and braising is that the former usually uses small pieces of meat and more liquid and the latter uses larger cuts and less liquid.) Both techniques are commonly used for tougher cuts of meat, such as pork shoulder or beef chuck. The cooking may take several hours, but that time is largely unattended and you are rewarded for your patience with deliciousness.

Even if an ingredient doesn't take hours to cook (as with chicken and sausage), it can still benefit from the two-step process: Brown the meat to give it color and develop a rich flavor base in the pot. Then add liquid, and let it all cook together slowly, allowing the flavors to meld in the process.

Cooking Tips

- Don't rush the browning of the meat. Heat oil in the pot, and add the meat in batches if necessary; crowding the pan can cause the meat to steam rather than brown. Don't move the meat until it's well browned; pieces are ready to turn (use tongs for this) when they release from the pan easily. Make sure you brown all sides unless the recipe specifies otherwise.

- While browning the meat, reduce the heat if the bottom of the pot is looking very dark. After browning a batch, if the bits in the pan look burned, wipe them out with a paper towel and add more oil.

- While cooking, the liquid should be at a bare simmer. This is often done on the stovetop, but a low oven (275° to 300°F) works, too. Even if a recipe specifies one method, you can always choose the other, depending on whether you want to free up a burner or oven space. Adjust the heat as necessary to achieve a simmer.

- Think ahead: Stews and braises usually taste even better a day or two after cooking, making them ideal for busy weeks or for entertaining.

EASY-TO-GRIP HANDLES
These pots are heavy empty, let alone when full. Make sure handles are comfortable to hold (even with oven mitts), so you can get a firm grip.

TIGHT-FITTING, HEATPROOF LID
This traps moisture, so slow-cooked dishes don't dry out. It needs to be able to take the heat of the oven.

CAST-IRON CONSTRUCTION
This metal heats evenly for searing and retains heat beautifully, for cooking over low temperatures without developing hot spots or causing food to burn. Coating the metal with colorful, glossy enamel makes it attractive, easy to maintain, and versatile (raw black cast iron can rust, and it reacts with acidic ingredients).

A NOTE ABOUT SIZE
A six- to eight-quart model is a good bet—big enough for a whole chicken or big batch of stew, but not unwieldy. Round versus oval is a matter of personal preference.

Beef Stew with Noodles

ACTIVE TIME 20 MINUTES · TOTAL TIME 1 HOUR

This beef stew has a couple of clever twists: The meat is cut into smaller pieces than often called for, shortening the cooking time, and the noodles cook right in the pot. SERVES 4

- 2 pounds boneless beef chuck, cut into ½-inch cubes
- Coarse salt and freshly ground pepper
- 2 tablespoons vegetable oil
- 1 medium yellow onion, sliced lengthwise
- 2 tablespoons all-purpose flour
- 5½ cups low-sodium chicken broth
- 3 cups water
- ½ pound carrots, cut into 1-inch pieces
- 2 medium russet potatoes, peeled and cut into 1-inch pieces
- 2 cups egg noodles
- 3 tablespoons finely chopped fresh flat-leaf parsley leaves
- 1 teaspoon red-wine vinegar

Season beef with salt and pepper. In a large Dutch oven, heat oil over high. Working in batches, add beef and cook until browned, about 6 minutes. Add onion and season with salt and pepper. Cook until onion begins to soften (reducing heat if necessary), about 5 minutes. Stir in flour, and cook 1 to 2 minutes. Add broth and the water, stirring and scraping up browned bits with a wooden spoon. Bring to a boil; then reduce to a simmer and cook until beef is tender, about 25 minutes.

Add carrots and potatoes; cook until potatoes are tender, about 10 minutes. Add noodles and cook until tender, about 8 minutes. Season with salt and pepper. Stir in parsley and vinegar just before serving.

BRIGHT IDEA
A dash of vinegar is a great finishing touch for rich dishes like this one: A little acidity really makes the whole dish shine. Try it on other stews and soups, too.

  DUTCH OVEN

Chicken and Dumplings

ACTIVE TIME 20 MINUTES · TOTAL TIME 45 MINUTES

Want to make people happy? Serve bowls of this down-home chicken stew with fluffy herb-flecked dumplings on a chilly day (actually, it would be welcome any day). SERVES 6

CHICKEN STEW

- 3 tablespoons unsalted butter
- 1 small yellow onion, minced
- 3 carrots, cut into ½-inch pieces
- 2 celery stalks, thinly sliced
- 2 teaspoons chopped fresh thyme leaves
- ⅓ cup all-purpose flour
- 3 cups low-sodium chicken broth
- 1¼ pounds boneless, skinless chicken breast, cut into ¾-inch pieces
- ½ pound green beans, trimmed and cut into 1-inch pieces

  Coarse salt and freshly ground pepper

DUMPLINGS

- 1 cup all-purpose flour
- 1 teaspoon baking powder
- 1 teaspoon coarse salt
- 2 tablespoons chopped fresh flat-leaf parsley leaves, plus more for garnish
- 2 tablespoons cold unsalted butter
- ½ cup whole milk

Make chicken stew: In a medium Dutch oven, melt butter over medium-high heat. Add onion, carrots, celery, and thyme; cook until onion is translucent, about 4 minutes. Add flour and cook, stirring, 1 minute. Gradually add broth, stirring constantly, and bring to a boil. Add chicken and return to a boil. Reduce heat and simmer 5 minutes. Stir in green beans; season with salt and pepper.

Meanwhile, make dumplings: Whisk together flour, baking powder, and salt; then whisk in parsley. With a pastry blender or two knives, cut in butter until mixture resembles coarse meal. Stir in milk with a fork just until a dough forms. Drop batter by heaping tablespoons on top of stew. Cover and simmer just until dumplings are cooked through, about 12 minutes. Garnish with chopped parsley.

Carnitas Tacos

ACTIVE TIME 15 MINUTES • TOTAL TIME 1 HOUR 15 MINUTES

This Mexican-style pork is made by simmering an inexpensive cut in water and then browning it. The method yields tender, crisp meat for serving with tortillas and toppings. MAKES 12 TACOS

---

2 pounds boneless pork shoulder, cut into 1½-inch pieces

Coarse salt and freshly ground pepper

12 corn or flour tortillas, toasted or warmed, for serving

1 small white onion, finely chopped, for serving

½ cup packed fresh cilantro leaves, for serving

Guacamole or diced avocado, for serving

Sour cream, for serving

Radishes, thinly sliced, for serving

Lime wedges, for serving

In a medium Dutch oven, cover pork with ½ inch water and bring to a rapid simmer over medium-high heat. Cook, turning pieces occasionally, until water evaporates, about 45 minutes. Season generously with salt and pepper. Continue to cook, turning pieces frequently, until crisp and browned on all sides, about 12 minutes. Transfer carnitas to a plate and serve with tortillas, onion, cilantro, guacamole or avocado, sour cream, sliced radishes, and lime wedges.

MAKING GUACAMOLE
Combine two mashed avocados and one minced jalapeño with chopped fresh cilantro, fresh lime juice, and salt and pepper to taste.

 DUTCH OVEN

ABOUT SAFFRON
The stigmas from crocus flowers—more commonly known as saffron—may be the world's most expensive spice, but just a pinch of the precious threads gives a dish like this an unmistakable color and fragrance.

Arroz con Pollo

ACTIVE TIME 25 MINUTES • TOTAL TIME 1 HOUR

Here's chicken and rice—with a Spanish accent. Variations on this dish are beloved throughout Spain and Latin America. This version is studded with green olives and infused with the heady flavors of wine, onion, garlic, bay leaves, and saffron. SERVES 6

½ cup dry white wine

Pinch of saffron threads

6 bone-in chicken thighs (about 6 ounces each)

Coarse salt and freshly ground pepper

2 tablespoons extra-virgin olive oil

1 large yellow onion, finely chopped

2 tablespoons minced garlic

1 large tomato, chopped

2 dried bay leaves

1½ cups short-grain rice, preferably Valencia

3 cups low-sodium chicken broth, plus more if needed

1 cup pimiento-stuffed green olives, drained

Preheat oven to 375°F. In a bowl, combine wine and saffron.

Season chicken with salt and pepper. In a large Dutch oven or braiser, heat oil over medium-high. Add chicken, skin-side down; cook until browned, 6 to 7 minutes. Flip and cook 2 minutes more; transfer to a plate.

Drain all but 2 tablespoons fat. Add onion and garlic; cook, stirring often, until translucent, 4 minutes. Add tomato and cook, stirring often, until softened, about 5 minutes. Stir in wine-saffron mixture, bay leaves, ½ teaspoon salt, and ¼ teaspoon pepper. Cook until wine is nearly evaporated, 5 to 8 minutes.

Stir in rice, broth, and olives. Nestle chicken into rice, skin-side up. Bring to a simmer, cover, and transfer to oven. Cook until liquid is absorbed and chicken is cooked through, 25 to 30 minutes. Let stand 10 minutes before serving.

Gigante Beans with Feta and Arugula

ACTIVE TIME 30 MINUTES · TOTAL TIME 2 HOURS 35 MINUTES, PLUS SOAKING

The Greek word for "giant" is a fitting name for these big beans, which become irresistibly creamy when cooked in a tomato-based sauce. If you can't find them, try lima beans instead. SERVES 4

- 8 ounces dried gigante beans
- 1 tablespoon extra-virgin olive oil, plus more for drizzling
- 1 large onion, finely chopped
- 2 garlic cloves, thinly sliced
- 2 tablespoons tomato paste
- 1 can (28 ounces) whole peeled tomatoes, drained and finely chopped
- 4½ cups water
- 1 tablespoon red-wine vinegar
  Coarse salt
- 1 bunch arugula (about 5 cups)
- ½ cup feta cheese, crumbled (2 ounces)
- 3 tablespoons coarsely chopped fresh dill

Cover beans with cold water, and let sit overnight; drain.

In a Dutch oven, heat oil over medium. Add onion and cook until soft, 8 to 10 minutes. Add garlic and tomato paste. Cook until fragrant, 2 to 3 minutes.

Add beans, tomatoes, and the water to pot. Bring to a boil; then reduce heat and just barely simmer, partially covered, until beans are tender, about 2 hours. Add vinegar and 1 teaspoon salt. Stir in arugula.

Serve topped with feta and dill and drizzled with oil.

One Pot, Four Ways
Pork Stew

ACTIVE TIME 20 MINUTES · TOTAL TIME 2 HOURS

Pork shoulder is among the best cuts for braising in a Dutch oven—and it's affordable, too. Pair it with different seasonal ingredients, and you can enjoy delicious stews year-round. SERVES 4

Pork Stew with Root Vegetables

1½ pounds pork shoulder, cut into 1-inch pieces

Coarse salt and freshly ground pepper

3 tablespoons olive oil

1 large leek (white and light-green parts only), cut into 1-inch pieces and rinsed well

3 garlic cloves, thinly sliced

3 sprigs thyme

2 tablespoons all-purpose flour

1½ cups hard apple cider

2½ cups low-sodium chicken broth

1 medium parsnip, peeled and cut into 1-inch pieces

½ small celery root, peeled and cut into ¾-inch pieces

½ small rutabaga, peeled and cut into ¾-inch pieces

¼ cup chopped fresh flat-leaf parsley leaves

1. Season pork with salt and pepper. In a small Dutch oven, heat 2 tablespoons oil over medium-high. Working in batches, add the pork and cook until browned, 5 to 7 minutes. Transfer to a plate. Add remaining tablespoon oil, the leek, garlic, and thyme; cook until the leek is translucent, about 3 minutes. Stir in flour and cook 1 minute.

2. Add cider and bring to a boil for 1 minute. Add broth and pork, and bring back to a boil. Reduce to a simmer; cook, partially covered, until pork is tender, about 1 hour and 15 minutes.

3. Add parsnip, celery root, and rutabaga, and return to a boil. Reduce to a simmer; cook, partially covered, until vegetables are tender, 25 to 30 minutes more.

4. Stir in parsley, and season with salt and pepper.

with Potatoes and Rosemary

- In step 1, replace leek with 1 sliced **onion** and 8 ounces quartered **button mushrooms.** Replace thyme with 2 sprigs **rosemary** and 2 teaspoons freshly ground **pepper.** Cook 7 minutes.

- In step 2, replace cider with 2 cups dry **red wine,** such as Cabernet Sauvignon. Reduce broth to 2 cups.

- In step 3, replace parsnip, celery root, and rutabaga with 1 pound **red or white potatoes,** peeled and cut into 1-inch pieces.

with Asparagus and Peas

- In step 1, omit thyme.

- In step 2, replace cider with dry **white wine,** such as Sauvignon Blanc. Cook pork for 1 hour and 35 minutes.

- In step 3, replace parsnip, celery root, and rutabaga with 1 bunch **asparagus,** cut into 1-inch pieces, and 1 cup fresh **peas** (if using frozen, see next step); cook only 5 minutes more.

- In step 4, replace parsley with 1 teaspoon chopped fresh **tarragon** (if using frozen peas, add them with the tarragon).

with Fennel and Olives

- In step 1, replace leek and thyme with 1 sliced **onion,** 1 teaspoon whole **fennel seeds,** and 1 dried **bay leaf.**

- In step 2, replace cider with dry **white wine,** such as Sauvignon Blanc. Replace broth with 1 can (28 ounces) whole peeled **tomatoes,** pureed with their juice.

- In step 3, replace parsnip, celery root, and rutabaga with 2 heads **fennel,** cut into 1-inch pieces, and 1 cup **Kalamata olives,** pitted.

PORK STEW
with Root Vegetables
PAGE 24

PORK STEW
with Potatoes
and Rosemary
PAGE 25

PORK STEW
with Asparagus
and Peas
PAGE 25

PORK STEW
with Fennel
and Olives
PAGE 25

Chicken Fricassee with Fennel and Artichoke

ACTIVE TIME 30 MINUTES • TOTAL TIME 55 MINUTES

Our fresh take on fricassee, a classic French stew, includes fennel and artichoke hearts for a chicken dinner that's as impressive and elegant as it is easy. SERVES 4 TO 6

---

1 whole chicken (about 4 pounds), cut into 10 pieces

Coarse salt and freshly ground pepper

1 tablespoon extra-virgin olive oil

1 fennel bulb, cut into ¼-inch wedges, fronds reserved

1 can (15 ounces) water-packed whole artichoke hearts, drained

1 small red onion, cut into ½-inch wedges

1 cup low-sodium chicken broth

1 tablespoon red-wine vinegar

3 tablespoons chopped fresh flat-leaf parsley leaves

Preheat oven to 425°F. Season chicken with 1 teaspoon salt and ½ teaspoon pepper. In a large Dutch oven, heat oil over high until hot but not smoking. Working in batches, brown chicken all over, 8 to 10 minutes; transfer to a plate. Pour off all but 1 tablespoon fat. Reduce heat to medium-high. Add fennel, artichokes, and onion, and brown, stirring occasionally, 2 to 3 minutes.

Return chicken to pot and add broth; transfer to oven. Braise until cooked through, 18 to 20 minutes. Transfer chicken and vegetables to a platter. Reduce cooking liquid over high heat to about ⅓ cup. Stir in vinegar. Pour sauce over chicken, and serve with fennel fronds and parsley.

Chicken-Tomatillo Stew

ACTIVE TIME 25 MINUTES • TOTAL TIME 55 MINUTES

When you're in the mood for Mexican, try this stew. It's made with tomatillos (similar to tomatoes, but with a green skin and a slightly tangy flavor), hominy, and cilantro. SERVES 4 TO 6

---

2 pounds tomatillos (husks removed), washed and halved

1 tablespoon vegetable oil

1 whole chicken (3 to 4 pounds), cut into 10 pieces (wings reserved for another use)

Coarse salt and freshly ground pepper

2 jalapeños, chopped, seeds removed if desired

½ medium white onion, chopped

3 garlic cloves, finely chopped

1 can (15 ounces) hominy, drained and rinsed

¼ cup chopped fresh cilantro leaves

In a food processor or blender, puree tomatillos. In a large Dutch oven, heat oil over medium-high. Season chicken with salt and pepper. Working in batches, add to pot, skin-side down, and cook until browned on one side, 6 minutes; transfer to a plate.

Add jalapeños and onion to pot; cook, stirring frequently, until slightly softened, 3 to 5 minutes. Add garlic and cook until fragrant, about 1 minute. Stir in tomatillo puree and hominy; season with salt and pepper. Nestle chicken, skin-side up, in sauce. Cover pot and simmer until chicken is cooked through, 22 to 25 minutes. Stir in cilantro; season with salt and pepper.

ABOUT HOMINY
Dried corn kernels that have been treated to remove their hulls, hominy is the signature element in the Mexican stew called posole (see page 188). You'll find canned hominy in supermarkets and Latin grocers.

Lamb and Apricot Stew

ACTIVE TIME 30 MINUTES · TOTAL TIME 1 HOUR 55 MINUTES

This is a take on a Moroccan tagine, a stew traditionally cooked in a clay pot of the same name—but a Dutch oven does the job nicely, too. Try serving this with couscous or flatbread. SERVES 4 TO 6

- 1 tablespoon olive oil
- 1½ pounds boneless lamb stew meat
    Coarse salt and freshly ground pepper
- 1 large yellow onion, halved and thinly sliced
- 4 garlic cloves, thinly sliced
- 1 can (14.5 ounces) diced tomatoes

- 1 two-inch piece fresh ginger, peeled and cut into matchsticks
- ¼ teaspoon ground cinnamon
- 2 cups water
- ¾ cup dried apricots
    Toasted sliced almonds, for serving

Preheat oven to 350°F. In a large Dutch oven, heat oil over medium-high. Season lamb with salt and pepper. Working in batches, add lamb and cook until browned, about 9 minutes; transfer to a plate.

Add onion and garlic to pot; cook until onion is softened, 5 minutes. Return lamb to pot, along with tomatoes (with their liquid), ginger, cinnamon, and the water; season with salt and pepper. Cover and transfer to oven; cook 45 minutes. Stir in apricots, cover, and cook until lamb is tender, 45 minutes more. Serve stew sprinkled with almonds.

DUTCH OVEN

Braised Chicken and Parsnips

ACTIVE TIME 20 MINUTES • TOTAL TIME 1 HOUR 15 MINUTES

Braise chicken in tangy cider vinegar with parsnips and sage for a dish you'll crave all fall and winter. We serve this over brown rice, but bread would also be great for soaking up the sauce. SERVES 4

- 8 bone-in, skinless chicken thighs (about 2 pounds)
  Coarse salt and freshly ground pepper
- 2 tablespoons vegetable oil
- 2 leeks (white and light-green parts only), thinly sliced and rinsed well
- ½ cup apple cider vinegar
- 1 pound parsnips, peeled and cut into 1-inch pieces
- 10 fresh sage leaves
- 1¾ cups low-sodium chicken broth

Preheat oven to 350°F. Season chicken with salt and pepper. In a medium Dutch oven, heat oil over medium-high. Working in batches, add chicken skin-side down and cook until browned, 8 to 10 minutes; transfer to a plate.

Reduce heat to medium. Add leeks and cook until tender, about 4 minutes. Add vinegar and scrape up brown bits with a wooden spoon. Add parsnips, sage, broth, and chicken (with its juices), and bring to a boil.

Cover and transfer to oven. Cook until parsnips are very tender and chicken is cooked through, about 50 minutes.

WASHING LEEKS
Leeks can have lots of dirt between their layers. To clean sliced rounds, place them in a bowl of cool water for a few minutes, swishing them around occasionally. Then lift them out of the water, leaving any dirt behind. Repeat as necessary until water is clean.

Sausage, Chicken, and White-Bean Gratin

ACTIVE TIME 40 MINUTES · TOTAL TIME 1 HOUR 10 MINUTES

The celebrated cassoulet of France inspired this sticks-to-your-ribs dish, which swaps chicken breast for the traditional duck or goose. Our big-batch recipe is great for a party. SERVES 10

- 1½ cups very coarse fresh breadcrumbs
- ¾ cup grated Parmigiano-Reggiano cheese
- 3 tablespoons chopped fresh flat-leaf parsley leaves
- 1 tablespoon plus 1 teaspoon chopped fresh thyme leaves
- 2 teaspoons chopped fresh rosemary
- 1 teaspoon thinly sliced fresh sage leaves
  Coarse salt and freshly ground pepper
- 4 ounces bacon (about 4 slices)

- 2 boneless, skinless chicken breast halves (about 1 pound total), cut into 1-inch cubes
- 1½ pounds sweet Italian sausage (casings removed), cut into ½-inch-thick pieces
- 4 garlic cloves, finely chopped
- 1 medium yellow onion, thinly sliced
- ½ cup dry white wine
- 2 cans (14.5 ounces each) cannellini beans, rinsed and drained
- 1 can (14.5 ounces) diced tomatoes, drained
- 1 cup low-sodium chicken broth

Preheat oven to 375°F. Combine breadcrumbs, cheese, 1 tablespoon each parsley and thyme, 1 teaspoon rosemary, and ½ teaspoon sage; season with salt and pepper. In a Dutch oven, cook bacon over medium heat until crisp, 5 to 7 minutes. Transfer to paper towels.

Add chicken to pot; cook until browned, about 6 minutes. Transfer to a plate. Add sausage and cook, stirring occasionally, until browned, about 5 minutes. Transfer to plate. Drain all but 2 tablespoons fat. Add garlic and onion; cook, stirring, until soft, about 3 minutes. Add wine and cook, scraping up brown bits with a wooden spoon, until most of the liquid has evaporated, about 2 minutes. Stir in chicken, sausage, beans, tomatoes, and broth, plus remaining 2 tablespoons parsley, 1 teaspoon each rosemary and thyme, and ½ teaspoon sage; season with salt and pepper. Sprinkle with breadcrumbs.

Cover pot; bake until bubbling, about 20 minutes. Uncover; bake until golden brown, about 10 minutes. Crumble reserved bacon on top. Let cool slightly before serving.

  DUTCH OVEN

ABOUT CHILI POWDER
Not to be confused with pure dried ground
chiles, chili powder is a blend of ingredients
usually containing dried chiles but also
cumin, garlic, and other spices. So it's no
wonder that each chili powder tastes
different. If you cook a lot of chili, try a few
brands to see which you like best.

Texas Red Chili

ACTIVE TIME 40 MINUTES · TOTAL TIME 3 HOURS 45 MINUTES

In the Lone Star State, chili is serious business, and the source of much debate. One thing the locals agree on: A bowl of hearty, spicy "Texas Red" is made with beef, and—most important—it never contains beans. SERVES 6 TO 8

- 3 pounds trimmed beef chuck, cut into 1-inch pieces
- Coarse salt and freshly ground pepper
- 3 tablespoons safflower or canola oil, plus more as needed
- 2 medium onions, coarsely chopped, plus more for serving
- 7 garlic cloves, minced

- 2 jalapeño or serrano chiles, seeded if desired, minced
- ½ cup chili powder
- 1 can (28 ounces) whole peeled plum tomatoes, pureed with their juice
- 4 cups water
- 2 to 3 teaspoons white vinegar, to taste
- Grated cheddar cheese, for serving

Season beef with 2½ teaspoons salt and ½ teaspoon pepper. In a medium Dutch oven, heat 2 tablespoons oil over medium-high. Working in batches, add beef and cook until browned, about 10 minutes per batch, adding more oil as needed; transfer to a plate.

Add remaining tablespoon oil, the onions, garlic, and chiles to pot; cook until onions are translucent, about 5 minutes. (If the pan gets too dark, add a little water, and scrape up browned bits with a wooden spoon.) Add chili powder; cook, stirring constantly, until fragrant, about 30 seconds.

Stir in beef, tomato puree, the water, and ½ teaspoon salt; bring to a boil. Reduce heat and simmer gently, partially covered, until meat is very tender and juices are thick, 2½ to 3 hours. (If chili seems dry, add a little water.) Season with salt, and stir in vinegar. Serve immediately, sprinkled with cheddar and onion.

Spanish-Style Chicken

ACTIVE TIME 30 MINUTES · TOTAL TIME 1 HOUR

For the most authentic taste, dust the chicken with pimentón dulce, or Spanish sweet smoked paprika. Piquillo peppers, sherry vinegar, and green olives add more layers of flavor. SERVES 4 TO 6

- 1 whole chicken (3½ to 4 pounds), cut into 10 pieces
- Coarse salt
- ½ teaspoon pimentón
- 1 tablespoon extra-virgin olive oil, plus more as needed
- 6 garlic cloves, minced
- 1 heaping tablespoon tomato paste
- ⅓ cup sherry vinegar
- 2 cups low-sodium chicken broth
- 6 jarred marinated piquillo peppers, cut into strips
- ½ cup green olives, such as Cerignola, pitted
- 2 tablespoons chopped fresh flat-leaf parsley leaves, for garnish

Preheat oven to 400°F. Season chicken with salt and pimentón. In a Dutch oven, heat oil over medium-high. Working in batches, add chicken skin-side down; cook until browned, 6 to 7 minutes, adding more oil as needed. Flip and cook 2 minutes more; transfer to a plate.

Reduce heat to low; stir in garlic and then tomato paste, scraping up browned bits with a wooden spoon. Return chicken to pan, increase heat to high, and pour in vinegar. Boil, stirring, until reduced to a glaze.

Stir in broth, and bring to a boil. Add peppers and olives. Transfer to oven and cook until chicken is just cooked through and liquid is reduced by half, 20 to 25 minutes. Garnish with parsley before serving.

Chicken with Creamy Corn and Bacon

ACTIVE TIME 30 MINUTES · TOTAL TIME 1 HOUR 15 MINUTES

Please the palate with a mix of flavors and textures: Chicken, couscous, bacon, and corn are all braised in milk for a silky finish. Arugula adds welcome color and crispness. SERVES 4

- 4 whole bone-in chicken legs

  Coarse salt and freshly ground pepper

- 2 tablespoons extra-virgin olive oil, plus more for drizzling

- 6 ounces thick-cut bacon (about 3 slices), cut into ½-inch pieces

- 1 medium yellow onion, finely chopped

- 1 head garlic, separated and left unpeeled

- ¾ cup Israeli, or pearl, couscous

- 2½ cups whole milk

- 3 sprigs thyme, plus 2 teaspoons leaves

- 1 cup frozen corn, thawed

- 2 ounces baby arugula (about 2 cups)

  Fresh lemon juice, for drizzling

Season chicken with salt and pepper. In a large Dutch oven, heat oil over medium-high. Working in batches, add chicken and cook until browned all over, about 7 minutes. Transfer chicken to a plate; discard fat. Add bacon to the pot; cook until crisp, 5 to 7 minutes. Drain all but 1 tablespoon fat. Add onion, garlic, and couscous; cook until couscous is golden, about 5 minutes.

Add milk and thyme sprigs, and bring to a simmer. Add chicken, skin-side up. Reduce heat, cover, and simmer 30 minutes. Stir in corn and thyme leaves; cover and cook until liquid is absorbed, 15 to 20 minutes. Divide couscous mixture among 4 plates. Top with chicken and arugula. Season with salt and pepper. Drizzle with lemon juice and oil before serving.

Cajun Stew

ACTIVE TIME 20 MINUTES · TOTAL TIME 50 MINUTES

This stew has all the trademark ingredients of Cajun cooking—andouille sausage, shrimp, cayenne pepper. It also begins with a roux and the "holy trinity" of onion, celery, and bell pepper. Serve with steamed rice or crusty bread, if you wish. SERVES 6

2 tablespoons vegetable oil

2 tablespoons all-purpose flour

1 red onion, thinly sliced

2 garlic cloves, minced

2 celery stalks, coarsely chopped

1 red or green bell pepper, coarsely chopped

¼ teaspoon cayenne pepper

Coarse salt

1 can (28 ounces) diced tomatoes

1½ cups water

¾ pound andouille or kielbasa, sliced into ½-inch-thick rounds

2 cups frozen sliced okra (from a 12-ounce package), thawed

½ pound large shrimp, peeled and deveined

Heat a braiser or medium Dutch oven over medium. Add oil and flour; cook, whisking constantly, until golden brown, 5 to 7 minutes. Add onion, garlic, celery, and bell pepper; cook until crisp-tender, about 7 minutes. Add cayenne and ½ teaspoon salt.

Stir in tomatoes (with their liquid), the water, and sausage. Bring to a boil, reduce to a simmer, and cook, partially covered, until slightly thickened, about 25 minutes. Add okra and simmer 3 minutes. Add shrimp and cook until opaque, 3 to 4 minutes more. Season with salt.

ABOUT OKRA
The green pods—which are botanically related to cotton—release a sticky substance as they cook, thickening stews like this one. You may see fresh okra in your store during the summer months (or year-round in the South), but frozen works just as well in this recipe.

Beer-Braised Sausages with Potatoes

ACTIVE TIME 35 MINUTES · TOTAL TIME 1 HOUR 15 MINUTES

If you've never cooked with beer, you may be surprised at how it reduces into a savory sauce. In this Oktoberfest-inspired recipe, turkey sausages can be used instead of the pork sausages. SERVES 4

---

2 tablespoons extra-virgin olive oil

1½ pounds pork sausages

1 medium yellow onion, thinly sliced

12 ounces pale ale

1½ pounds small red potatoes, scrubbed and halved

2 cups water

Coarse salt and freshly ground pepper

1 tablespoon red-wine vinegar

2 tablespoons chopped fresh flat-leaf parsley leaves

In a large Dutch oven, heat 1 tablespoon oil over medium-high. Add sausages and cook until browned on all sides, about 8 minutes. Add onion and cook until softened, about 7 minutes. Add ale, potatoes, and the water; season with salt and pepper, and press down potatoes to submerge in cooking liquid. Bring to a boil; then cover, reduce heat to medium, and cook until potatoes are tender, about 20 minutes.

Transfer sausages to a serving platter and keep warm. In a large bowl, stir together remaining tablespoon oil, the vinegar, and parsley. With a slotted spoon, transfer potato mixture to dressing (reserve cooking liquid), and toss to combine.

Return pot to high heat, and boil cooking liquid until reduced to 1 cup, about 12 minutes. Add potatoes to serving platter with sausages; drizzle half the reduced cooking liquid over top. Serve sausages and potatoes with remaining cooking liquid on the side.

Baked Risotto with Carrots and Squash

ACTIVE TIME 20 MINUTES · TOTAL TIME 50 MINUTES

Arborio rice studded with red lentils and fall vegetables makes a colorful and appealing meatless main course. Leftovers—should there be any—are perfect for lunch the next day. SERVES 4

- 2 tablespoons vegetable oil
- 1 small onion, finely diced
- 4 garlic cloves, minced
- 2 tablespoons minced peeled fresh ginger
- 1 teaspoon ground cumin
  Coarse salt

- 3 medium carrots, cut on a diagonal into ¾-inch slices (2 cups)
- 1 cup Arborio rice
- ½ cup red lentils, picked over and rinsed
- 2½ cups water
- ½ small butternut squash, peeled, seeded, and cut into 1-inch chunks
  Lime wedges and fresh cilantro sprigs, for serving

Preheat oven to 400°F. In a medium Dutch oven, heat oil over medium-high. Add onion, garlic, ginger, cumin, and 1½ teaspoons salt; cook until onion is translucent, about 3 minutes. Add carrots, rice, and lentils; cook, stirring, 1 minute. Add the water, and bring to a boil. Add squash and return to a boil. Cover and transfer to oven. Cook until liquid is absorbed and rice is tender, about 20 minutes. Let sit, covered, 10 minutes before serving. Squeeze with lime wedge, and top with cilantro before serving.

TRY IT WITH BROTH
We used water in this dish to keep it meat-free, but you can opt for chicken broth instead. It will give the meal a slightly deeper flavor.

 DUTCH OVEN

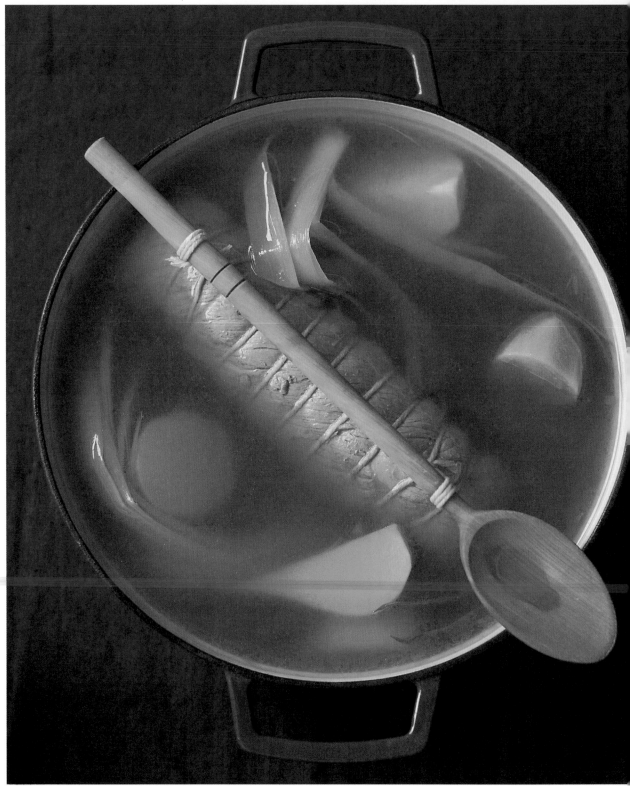

Beef on a String

ACTIVE TIME 50 MINUTES · TOTAL TIME 2 HOURS

Whether you call it by its French name, *boeuf à la ficelle,* or by the winsome English translation, this poached beef tenderloin is the perfect dinner-party dish. Ladle the cooking liquid over slices of beef and chunks of turnips, rutabaga, and potatoes. SERVES 6 TO 8

---

1 beef tenderloin (2 pounds), trimmed and tied

2 tablespoons extra-virgin olive oil

3 onions, finely diced

1 cup dry white wine

2 leeks, trimmed and halved lengthwise, rinsed well

1 turnip, peeled and cut into 1-inch wedges

½ rutabaga, peeled and cut into ¾-inch wedges

10 cups water

4 small potatoes, peeled and halved crosswise

Coarse salt and freshly ground pepper

Store-bought prepared horseradish and beets, for serving

Tie kitchen string to end ties on beef; secure to a wooden spoon long enough to balance on the rim of a Dutch oven. (The beef should not touch the bottom of the pot.) Set aside.

Heat oil in the pot over medium-high. Add onions; cook, stirring occasionally, until golden brown, about 20 minutes. (If mixture gets dry, add a few tablespoons water.) Add wine; cook, stirring, until almost evaporated, about 4 minutes. Add leeks, turnip, rutabaga, and the water. Bring to a simmer, then partially cover and cook at a bare simmer for 30 minutes. Transfer turnips to a dish. Continue cooking at bare simmer until rutabaga are fork-tender, about 10 minutes; transfer rutabaga to the dish.

Add beef to pot, with spoon on pot's rim. If necessary, add warm water to cover. Add potatoes; bring to a simmer. Adjust heat to maintain liquid temperature at 190°F, and cook until an instant-read thermometer inserted in beef reads 120°F, for rare, about 30 minutes. Meat will continue to cook after poaching. Transfer potatoes to the dish. Let beef rest, tented with foil, 5 minutes. Keep poaching liquid warm. Remove strings from beef and cut roast into slices. Strain broth through fine-mesh sieve. Divide broth, vegetables, and beef among bowls. Season with salt and pepper, and top with horseradish and beets.

Skillet & Sauté Pan

Talk about multitaskers: Skillets and sauté pans are the ones to reach for when you want to sear, sauté, scramble, or stir-fry, and even roast or bake. They make it easy to turn out a wide variety of meals.

The Basics

The terms *skillet* and *sauté pan* are often used interchangeably—and in fact the pans can be, too, though there are differences to their shapes. Skillets are slope-sided, and sauté pans are straight-sided. You can use these pans for many different kinds of recipes, as you'll see on the pages that follow. But in terms of classic culinary techniques, both pans excel at sautéing, or cooking food quickly in oil over direct heat; the term comes from the French verb "to jump," a reference to the way the food jumps when the pan is shaken. When you sauté, brown bits develop in the bottom of the pan. Add liquid and scrape up those bits (a process known as deglazing) to add intense flavor to your dish.

A cast-iron skillet is in a class by itself. This metal heats thoroughly and evenly and then holds the heat beautifully, which makes it our favorite choice, hands down, for getting a good sear on foods like pork chops. Cast iron isn't perfect, however: It reacts with acidic ingredients, such as tomatoes and wine, often giving food a metallic taste. If not seasoned (see opposite), the metal can rust. Fortunately, the more you use the pan, the better the seasoning.

Cooking Tips

- When sautéing, make sure you heat the oil well before adding ingredients to the pan. If the oil is cold, the food will absorb it. Crowding the pan can cause food to steam rather than sauté; cook in batches if necessary.

- The best cuts for sautéing and stir-frying are tender and of an even size and thickness. Bring the ingredients to room temperature first.

- A note about nonstick pans: These coatings are undeniably convenient for some dishes—think eggs—and make cleanup a breeze. But they don't let foods brown as much or develop flavorful bits in the pan, and many are not ovenproof, so they are not the most versatile choice.

- Stir-frying is traditionally done in a wok, but high heat is more important than the pan shape in this fast-cooking technique. A skillet or sauté pan (especially cast iron) makes a fine substitute.

- If a recipe calls for covering the pan but your skillet doesn't have a lid, place a piece of parchment-lined foil over the top and then add a slightly larger lid.

Key Features

It's worth investing in heavy-duty ovenproof pans that conduct heat well and won't warp over high heat. A ten- or twelve-inch pan is a workhorse; a larger pan comes in handy when cooking for four or more people. Pans are measured across the top, so a slope-sided pan has less cooking area than a straight-sided one. Look for long, comfortable handles that feel balanced with the size of the pan. They should stay cool on the stovetop, but be ovenproof. Riveted handles are sturdiest.

SKILLET
The sloped sides make it easy to move ingredients in the pan (nothing gets stuck in the corners), and to turn out dishes like frittatas.

SAUTÉ PAN
Straight sides mean that broth and other liquids aren't likely to spill over when you're stirring, making these pans good for braising as well as sautéing. They often come with a lid (another bonus for braising) and have a looped handle opposite the main handle.

SEASONING A CAST-IRON SKILLET
New pans are often sold pre-seasoned. But if you have one in its raw, gray form, coat it with vegetable oil and bake it in a 300-degree oven for an hour, with a baking pan underneath to catch any drips. For cleaning, the key is to remove food but not the pan's seasoning. Conventional wisdom says to scrub with water and a brush, or some salt; if you can't bear the idea of not using soap, a little mild dishwashing liquid is fine. Dry the pan well (you can do this over a low burner), and rub it lightly with vegetable oil before putting it away.

Pork Chops with Warm Escarole Salad

ACTIVE TIME 25 MINUTES · TOTAL TIME 25 MINUTES

Try this update on pork chops and applesauce—with a few extra good-for-you ingredients. Here the apples are julienned and tossed with nutty chickpeas and wilted escarole. SERVES 4

- 4 bone-in pork chops (about 9 ounces each)

  Coarse salt and freshly ground pepper

- 2 tablespoons extra-virgin olive oil

- 1 cup canned chickpeas, drained and rinsed

- 1 pound escarole, leaves torn

- 1 medium apple, preferably Gala, cored and cut into matchsticks

- 1 tablespoon finely grated lemon zest, plus 1 teaspoon fresh lemon juice

Season pork chops with 1½ teaspoons salt and some pepper. In a large sauté pan, heat oil over medium-high. Add pork chops. Reduce heat to medium, and cook until browned on both sides and cooked through, 7 to 8 minutes total. Transfer chops to a plate.

Add chickpeas to pan, and cook for 2 minutes. Working in batches, add escarole and cook, stirring, adding more as the leaves wilt. Sprinkle with ½ teaspoon salt, and season with pepper. Remove pan from heat, and stir in apple and lemon zest and juice. Serve with chops.

ZESTING CITRUS
A rasp-style grater is the quickest and easiest tool for removing the zest. If you don't have that type of grater, use a paring knife or vegetable peeler to remove the zest in strips, and then finely chop it.

Linguine with Tomato and Basil

ACTIVE TIME 15 MINUTES · TOTAL TIME 20 MINUTES

You won't believe it till you try it: Cook linguine in water with tomato, basil, and garlic thrown right in the same pot. Let the water boil away, and you have pasta in a delectable sauce. SERVES 4

12 ounces linguine

12 ounces cherry or grape tomatoes, halved or quartered if large

1 onion, thinly sliced

4 garlic cloves, thinly sliced

½ teaspoon red-pepper flakes

2 sprigs basil, plus torn leaves for garnish

2 tablespoons extra-virgin olive oil, plus more for serving

Coarse salt and freshly ground pepper

4½ cups water

Freshly grated Parmigiano-Reggiano cheese, for serving

In a large sauté pan, combine pasta, tomatoes, onion, garlic, red-pepper flakes, basil, oil, 2 teaspoons salt, ¼ teaspoon pepper, and the water; bring to a boil over high heat. Cook pasta, stirring frequently with tongs, until al dente and water has nearly evaporated, about 9 minutes.

Season with salt and pepper, and garnish with torn basil. Serve with oil and cheese.

Beef-and-Pineapple Red Curry

ACTIVE TIME 30 MINUTES · TOTAL TIME 30 MINUTES

Red curry paste, a jarred blend of chiles and other seasonings, is a fantastic ingredient to keep in your pantry. Combined with coconut milk, it makes a quick sauce for a Thai-style curry. SERVES 4

- 1 tablespoon vegetable oil
- ¼ cup red curry paste
- 1 pound sirloin steak, trimmed and cut against the grain into very thin strips
- ½ pound green beans, trimmed and cut in half crosswise
- 12 ounces pineapple, cut into 1-inch cubes
- 1½ cups low-sodium chicken broth
- 1 cup unsweetened coconut milk
- ½ cup fresh basil leaves, torn

In a large skillet or wok, heat oil over medium-high. Add curry paste and cook, stirring, until fragrant, 30 seconds. Add steak and cook, stirring, until browned, 2 minutes. Add green beans and pineapple; cook, stirring, until pineapple starts to release juices, 1 minute. Add broth and coconut milk, and bring to a boil. Reduce heat and cook at a rapid simmer until green beans are crisp-tender, 8 minutes. Garnish with basil before serving.

PEELING A PINEAPPLE
To remove the skin from this prickly fruit, slice off the top and bottom. Stand the pineapple on end, and slice off the peel in strips, following the curve of the fruit. Quarter the peeled pineapple. Stand the quarters on end, and slice out the cores. Cut quarters in half lengthwise. Slice into wedges or cubes.

Shrimp with Tomatoes and Orzo

ACTIVE TIME 15 MINUTES • TOTAL TIME 35 MINUTES

Keep frozen shrimp on hand, and dinners that feel special can be everyday affairs. The crustacean pairs perfectly with tomatoes and basil. SERVES 4

- 2 tablespoons extra-virgin olive oil
- 6 garlic cloves, minced
- 3 cups halved grape tomatoes
  Coarse salt and freshly ground pepper
- ¾ pound orzo
- 3¼ cups low-sodium chicken broth
- 1 pound large shrimp, peeled and deveined
- 1 cup fresh basil leaves, torn

Preheat oven to 400°F, with a rack in top position. In a large ovenproof skillet with a tight-fitting lid, heat 1 tablespoon plus 2 teaspoons oil over medium. Add garlic and cook until just beginning to brown, 1 minute. Increase heat to high and add tomatoes; season with salt and pepper. Cook, stirring occasionally, until softened, 6 minutes. Add orzo and broth, and bring to a simmer. Cover and bake until liquid is mostly absorbed, 10 to 12 minutes.

Toss shrimp with remaining teaspoon oil and ¼ teaspoon each salt and pepper. Remove skillet from oven, and place shrimp on top of orzo. Heat broiler. Broil until shrimp are opaque throughout, 4 minutes. Sprinkle with basil and serve.

THAWING FROZEN SHRIMP
Place shrimp in the refrigerator to thaw overnight. Too late for that? Put them in a colander, and run cold water over them until they thaw. It should take five to ten minutes.

Braised Chicken with Potatoes and Lemon

ACTIVE TIME 10 MINUTES · TOTAL TIME 40 MINUTES

Here's an easy chicken dinner with a Mediterranean spin. Adding a bit of cornstarch at the end turns the lemony cooking liquid into a silky sauce. SERVES 4 TO 6

---

6 bone-in chicken thighs (about 2¼ pounds)

Coarse salt

1 tablespoon extra-virgin olive oil

1¼ cups low-sodium chicken broth

12 ounces fingerling potatoes or halved new potatoes

5 garlic cloves, smashed and peeled

½ cup large green olives, such as Cerignola, pitted

1 small lemon, cut into wedges

6 sprigs thyme

1 teaspoon cornstarch

Preheat oven to 450°F. Season chicken with salt. In a large, heavy ovenproof skillet, heat oil over medium-high. Add chicken, skin-side down, and cook until browned, about 5 minutes. Flip chicken and push to side of skillet. Add 1 cup broth and ½ teaspoon salt. Add potatoes to liquid, and bring to a boil. Add garlic, olives, lemon wedges, and thyme, and return to a boil.

Transfer skillet to oven. Roast, stirring potatoes halfway through, until potatoes are tender and chicken is cooked through, about 30 minutes.

Return skillet to stove. Mix cornstarch with remaining ¼ cup broth, and stir into pan. Bring to a boil to thicken sauce. Serve immediately.

SWAP IT
We used chicken thighs, which take roughly the same time to cook as the potatoes. But chicken breasts will work, too; just remove the pieces after about twenty minutes, and keep them warm while the potatoes finish cooking.

Mushroom-Cheddar Frittata

ACTIVE TIME 30 MINUTES · TOTAL TIME 40 MINUTES

We reimagined eggs and toast, baking cubes of sourdough right into a cheesy frittata. It would be good any time of day—after all, who doesn't love breakfast for dinner? SERVES 4

10 large eggs, lightly beaten

¼ cup whole milk

Coarse salt and freshly ground pepper

2 tablespoons unsalted butter

2 thick slices sourdough bread, cut into ¾-inch cubes

½ pound button mushrooms, trimmed and sliced

6 scallions, white and green parts separated and thinly sliced

½ cup shredded cheddar cheese (2 ounces)

Preheat oven to 425°F. In a bowl, whisk together eggs and milk; season with salt and pepper. In a 10-inch nonstick ovenproof skillet, melt 1 tablespoon butter over medium-high heat. Add bread; cook, turning, until golden, about 4 minutes. Transfer to a plate.

Add remaining tablespoon butter and the mushrooms, and cook until softened, about 4 minutes. Lower heat to medium, add scallion whites, and cook until soft, 3 minutes more; season with salt and pepper. Add egg mixture to skillet, stirring until large curds form and eggs are halfway set, 2 to 4 minutes. Press bread into eggs.

Sprinkle with cheddar, and bake until puffed and center is just set, 5 to 7 minutes. Top with scallion greens and serve.

MORE COMBOS
Mushrooms and cheddar are great together, but you can pair other favorite vegetables and cheeses, such as asparagus and Gruyère or bell peppers and Monterey Jack.

Turkey Skillet Pie

ACTIVE TIME 30 MINUTES · TOTAL TIME 50 MINUTES

This may become the new most-requested recipe in your house: Cheddar-buttermilk biscuits are dropped and baked over turkey chili for a guaranteed hit. SERVES 6 TO 8

---

1 cup all-purpose flour

1 teaspoon baking powder

¼ teaspoon baking soda

Coarse salt and freshly ground pepper

1 tablespoon vegetable oil

1 red bell pepper, thinly sliced

1 medium white onion, thinly sliced

8 ounces button mushrooms, trimmed and sliced

1½ pounds ground turkey, preferably dark meat

2 tablespoons tomato paste

1 tablespoon chili powder

1 can (14.5 ounces) diced tomatoes

3 tablespoons unsalted butter

⅓ cup buttermilk

1½ cups grated cheddar cheese (6 ounces)

Preheat oven to 425°F. In a bowl, whisk together flour, baking powder, baking soda, and ¼ teaspoon salt.

In a large, heavy ovenproof skillet, heat oil over medium-high. Add bell pepper, onion, and mushrooms. Cook, stirring, until tender, 8 to 10 minutes. Season with salt and pepper. Add turkey, tomato paste, and chili powder to skillet. Cook, stirring, until meat is no longer pink, about 3 minutes. Add tomatoes (with liquid); cook until some of the liquid has reduced, about 3 minutes. Season with salt and pepper. Remove from heat.

Cut butter into flour mixture with a pastry cutter or two knives until mixture resembles coarse meal. Stir in buttermilk and cheddar just until incorporated. Divide batter into 9 pieces, and place on top of turkey mixture. Bake until biscuits are golden brown, about 20 minutes.

One Pot, Four Ways
Macaroni and Cheese

ACTIVE TIME 40 MINUTES • TOTAL TIME 40 MINUTES

It's hard to improve on mac and cheese—but we think we've done it, by cooking the pasta right in the sauce. With a classic and three variations, there's something for every craving. SERVES 8

Skillet Macaroni and Cheese

- 6 tablespoons unsalted butter
- 1 cup fresh breadcrumbs
- ¼ cup grated Parmigiano-Reggiano cheese (1 ounce)
- 1 small yellow onion, finely chopped
- ½ cup all-purpose flour
- 6 cups milk, preferably 2 percent

- ¾ pound elbow macaroni
- 3 cups grated sharp white cheddar cheese (9 ounces)
- 1 cup grated Gruyère cheese (3 ounces)
- 1 teaspoon Dijon mustard
- Coarse salt and freshly ground pepper

1. Heat broiler. In a large, heavy ovenproof skillet, melt butter over medium-high heat. Remove 1 tablespoon butter, and combine with breadcrumbs and Parmigiano-Reggiano in a bowl.

2. Add onion to skillet, and cook until softened, 4 minutes. Whisk in flour; cook, stirring, 1 minute. Whisk in milk gradually; bring to a simmer. Add macaroni and cook, stirring constantly and scraping bottom of pan, until tender, about 6 minutes. Remove from heat, stir in cheddar, Gruyère, and mustard; season with salt and pepper. Top with breadcrumb mixture. Broil until golden brown, 1 to 2 minutes.

with Mushrooms and Fontina

In step 2, replace the onion with 8 ounces trimmed and sliced **cremini mushrooms.** Replace cheddar with grated **fontina cheese.** Replace mustard with 2 teaspoons chopped fresh **thyme** leaves.

with Spring Vegetables and Goat Cheese

In step 2, replace onion with 2 large **leeks** (white and light-green parts only), thinly sliced and rinsed well. After whisking in milk, add 2 cups thinly sliced **mixed vegetables,** such as **asparagus, carrots,** and **snap peas.** Replace Gruyère with 4 ounces crumbled **goat cheese.** Omit mustard.

with Bacon and Gouda

In step 2, omit onion. Replace cheddar with grated **Gouda cheese.** Stir in 8 slices cooked **bacon,** crumbled, when you add the cheese.

**SKILLET MACARONI
AND CHEESE**
PAGE 70

SKILLET MACARONI
with Mushrooms and Fontina
PAGE 71

SKILLET MACARONI
with Spring Vegetables
and Goat Cheese
PAGE 71

SKILLET MACARONI
with Bacon and Gouda
PAGE 71

Striped Bass with Clams and Corn

ACTIVE TIME 30 MINUTES · TOTAL TIME 30 MINUTES

Stop at the fish market then the farm stand, and you're well on your way to a fresh peak-of-summer dinner. Today's catch: mild, tender fish fillets in a brothy bowl of clams, zucchini, and corn. SERVES 4

- 2 tablespoons unsalted butter
- 1 small yellow onion, minced
- 3 garlic cloves, thinly sliced
  Coarse salt and freshly ground pepper
- 2 Yukon Gold potatoes, peeled and cut into ½-inch pieces
- 1¼ cups low-sodium chicken broth

- 12 small littleneck clams, scrubbed
- 2 cups corn kernels
- 1 small zucchini, sliced ¼-inch thick
- 4 skinless striped bass fillets (1 pound total), 1 inch thick, or other firm-fleshed white fish, such as sea bass or halibut
  Fresh basil leaves, for serving

In a large sauté pan, melt butter over medium-high heat. Add onion, garlic, and ½ teaspoon salt; sauté until translucent, about 3 minutes. Add potatoes and broth, and bring to a boil; cover and cook for 5 minutes. Add clams and cook, covered, 5 minutes. Stir in corn and zucchini, then push clams aside and nestle fish in pan. Cover and cook until clams are open and fish is opaque, 4 to 6 minutes. (Discard any unopened clams.) Serve topped with basil.

Savory Sausage and Tomato Pudding

ACTIVE TIME 10 MINUTES • TOTAL TIME 40 MINUTES

The British name of this dish—toad in the hole—will bring smiles to the dinner table. So will bites of the pudding, which is similar to a popover; it browns and puffs in the oven. SERVES 4

1½ cups all-purpose flour

1½ cups milk

3 large eggs

2 tablespoons unsalted butter, melted

1 teaspoon coarse salt

1 tablespoon extra-virgin olive oil

1 pound sausage, preferably Cumberland

5 whole scallions

10 cherry tomatoes, on the vine optional

Preheat oven to 425°F. In a blender, combine flour, milk, eggs, butter, and salt. In a 10-inch ovenproof skillet, heat oil over medium-high. Add sausage and scallions; cook until browned, about 5 minutes. Pour batter over sausages, and top with tomatoes. Bake until puffed and set, about 30 minutes. Serve immediately.

Spinach Pie

ACTIVE TIME 25 MINUTES · TOTAL TIME 55 MINUTES

In this streamlined version of Greek spanakopita, golden, flaky phyllo dough tops a savory spinach-and-feta filling. Frozen spinach is a time-saver; just make sure you squeeze out as much moisture as you can so the finished dish isn't soggy. SERVES 4

---

4 tablespoons unsalted butter

1 small yellow onion, chopped

20 ounces frozen chopped spinach, thawed and squeezed dry

1 cup whole-milk ricotta cheese (8 ounces)

3 large eggs

¼ cup crumbled feta cheese (1 ounce)

2 tablespoons chopped fresh dill

Coarse salt and freshly ground pepper

4 sheets frozen phyllo dough, thawed

Preheat oven to 375°F. In a 10-inch nonstick ovenproof skillet, melt butter over medium heat. Transfer 2 tablespoons to a bowl. Add onion to skillet; cook, stirring, until softened, 5 minutes. Remove from heat, and let cool slightly. Stir in spinach, ricotta, eggs, feta, dill, 1 teaspoon salt, and ¼ teaspoon pepper.

Lay 1 sheet phyllo on a work surface, and lightly brush with reserved melted butter. Lay over spinach mixture, folding edges under to fit inside skillet. (Keep extra phyllo covered while you work.) One at a time, brush remaining 3 sheets and add to skillet, rotating and scrunching each sheet slightly so edges are offset and top is ruffled. Transfer skillet to oven, and bake until golden brown and heated through, about 30 minutes.

WORKING WITH PHYLLO
You'll find this multilayered pastry (pronounced FEE-lo) in the freezer case. The paper-thin layers dry out quickly, so most recipes call for keeping extra sheets covered with a damp towel as you work. Brushing each layer with butter adds moisture and helps the pastry crisp up in the oven.

Stir-Fried Chicken with Bok Choy

ACTIVE TIME 20 MINUTES · TOTAL TIME 20 MINUTES

Instead of ordering takeout, try this super-speedy stir-fry. The mix of chicken and greens is satisfying on its own, but you can serve it with rice to soak up the delicious juices. SERVES 4

- ¼ cup low-sodium soy sauce
- 1 tablespoon rice vinegar (unseasoned)
- 2 teaspoons light-brown sugar
- 3 tablespoons water
- 2 boneless, skinless chicken breast halves (about 1 pound total), sliced into strips
- 1 tablespoon plus 1 teaspoon cornstarch

- 2 tablespoons vegetable oil
- 2 garlic cloves, thinly sliced
- 2 teaspoons minced peeled fresh ginger
- 4 cups sliced bok choy (from 1 head)
- 1 small red chile or jalapeño, seeded and sliced

In a bowl, combine soy sauce, vinegar, brown sugar, and the water.

In another bowl, toss chicken with cornstarch until coated. In a large sauté pan or wok, heat oil, garlic, and ginger over medium-high until fragrant, about 1 minute. Add chicken in a single layer, pressing against pan to sear. Cook, stirring, until lightly browned and just cooked through, 6 to 8 minutes.

Add bok choy and chile; cook, stirring, until bok choy wilts slightly, about 1 minute. Add soy sauce mixture; cook, stirring, until sauce thickens slightly, 2 minutes.

STIR-FRY SUCCESS
In restaurants, stir-frying is done in extra-large woks over very high heat. To approximate the effect at home, don't stack the meat in the pan, and make sure the pan and oil are nice and hot before you add the chicken.

Beet Hash with Eggs

ACTIVE TIME 30 MINUTES · TOTAL TIME 30 MINUTES

A new ingredient can transform a familiar recipe: Beets bring sweetness and a rosy color to meat-free hash. The hearty dish would be welcome on the brunch or dinner table. SERVES 4

- 1 pound beets, peeled and diced
- ½ pound Yukon Gold potatoes, scrubbed and diced
-    Coarse salt and freshly ground pepper
- 2 tablespoons extra-virgin olive oil
- 1 small onion, diced
- 2 tablespoons chopped fresh flat-leaf parsley leaves
- 4 large eggs

In a skillet or large sauté pan, cover beets and potatoes with water and bring to a boil. Season with salt; cook until tender, about 7 minutes. Drain and wipe out pan.

In the same pan, heat oil over medium-high. Add drained beets and potatoes; cook until potatoes begin to turn golden, about 4 minutes. Reduce heat to medium and add onion; cook, stirring, until tender, about 4 minutes. Season with salt and pepper, and stir in parsley.

Make 4 wide wells in the hash. Crack 1 egg into each, and season with salt. Cook until whites are set but yolks are still runny, 5 to 6 minutes.

BUYING BEETS
Smaller beets are more tender than large ones. Look for beets with the greens still attached, as the greens are delicious sautéed with a little garlic and olive oil.

Baked Rice with Sausage and Broccoli Rabe

ACTIVE TIME 20 MINUTES · TOTAL TIME 50 MINUTES

A skillet of rice makes a delectable starting point for a meal, as it can be combined with all kinds of ingredients. Broccoli rabe and sausage is one of our favorite pairings. SERVES 4

- 2 tablespoons extra-virgin olive oil
- 8 ounces Italian sausage, casings removed, broken into pieces
- ½ cup finely chopped yellow onion
- 3 garlic cloves, minced
- 1¼ cups Arborio rice
- ¼ cup dry white wine, such as Sauvignon Blanc
- 2¼ cups low-sodium chicken broth
- 1 bunch broccoli rabe (about 6 ounces), cut into 2-inch pieces, tossed with 1 tablespoon water and ¼ teaspoon coarse salt

Preheat oven to 400°F. In a large, heavy ovenproof skillet, heat oil over medium-high. Cook sausage, stirring often, until opaque, about 3 minutes. Stir in onion and garlic. Cook until translucent, about 3 minutes.

Stir in rice to coat, then wine; bring to a boil. Cook until rice absorbs almost all the liquid, 1 minute. Add broth; bring to a boil.

Transfer skillet to oven. Bake for 10 minutes. Add broccoli rabe. Bake until rice absorbs all the liquid, about 10 minutes. Remove from oven and stir. Let stand, covered, for 10 minutes before serving.

Spanish Baked Rice

ACTIVE TIME 15 MINUTES • TOTAL TIME 45 MINUTES

Here's another take on skillet rice: a pared-down version of paella with briny clams and spicy Spanish sausage. Be sure to buy the clams the day you plan to use them. SERVES 4

2 tablespoons extra-virgin olive oil

3 ounces dried chorizo, sliced ¼ inch thick

½ cup finely chopped yellow onion

3 garlic cloves, minced

1¼ cups Arborio rice

¼ cup dry white wine, such as Sauvignon Blanc

1½ cups low-sodium chicken broth

¾ cup water

12 littleneck clams, scrubbed well

Preheat oven to 400°F. In a large, heavy ovenproof skillet, heat oil over medium-high. Cook chorizo, stirring often, until edges are browned, about 2 minutes. Stir in onion and garlic. Cook until translucent, about 3 minutes.

Stir in rice to coat, then wine; bring to a boil. Cook until rice absorbs almost all the liquid, 1 minute. Add broth and the water; bring to a boil.

Transfer skillet to oven. Bake for 10 minutes. Add clams. Bake until clams open and rice absorbs all the liquid, about 10 minutes. (Discard any unopened clams.) Remove from oven, and let stand, covered, for 10 minutes before serving.

ABOUT CHORIZO
Dried chorizo, used in this dish, has been cured; it is available in large grocery stores. If you end up with extra, try it in soups, stews, tacos, and scrambled eggs.

Spanish Baked Rice
PAGE 85

Baked Rice with Sausage
and Broccoli Rabe
PAGE 84

Curried Chicken Potpie

ACTIVE TIME 25 MINUTES · TOTAL TIME 1 HOUR 25 MINUTES

Simplicity and spice: That's what sets apart this version of the comfort-food classic. A sheet of store-bought puff pastry means it's a cinch to assemble—and looks dramatic at the table. SERVES 4

- 1 sheet frozen puff pastry (from a 17.3-ounce package), thawed
- ¼ cup all-purpose flour, plus more for surface
- 3 tablespoons unsalted butter
- 1 large leek (white and light-green parts only), cut into ½-inch half-moons and rinsed well
- 4 parsnips, cut into 1-inch pieces
- 2 carrots, cut into 1-inch pieces

- Coarse salt and freshly ground pepper
- 3 cups low-sodium chicken broth
- 1 russet potato, peeled and cut into matchsticks
- 1 tablespoon plus 1 teaspoon curry powder
- 1 pound boneless, skinless chicken thighs, cut into 1-inch pieces
- 1 cup frozen peas
- 1 tablespoon milk

Preheat oven to 400°F. Unfold puff pastry onto a lightly floured baking sheet and roll out into an 11-by-12-inch rectangle; chill until firm, 15 to 30 minutes.

Meanwhile, in a large sauté pan or skillet, melt butter over medium-high heat. Add leek, parsnips, carrots, and 1 teaspoon salt; cook, stirring frequently, until slightly soft, 3 to 5 minutes. Add flour; cook, stirring, until golden, 1 to 2 minutes. Whisking constantly, stir in broth, potato, and curry powder. Bring to a boil; then reduce heat and simmer very gently until potato is tender, stirring occasionally, 8 to 10 minutes. Season with salt and pepper. Let cool completely. Stir in chicken and peas.

Top chicken mixture with pastry (trim to fit, if necessary). With a paring knife, cut an X in the center to vent steam. Brush pastry with milk. Bake potpie 15 minutes, then tent edges with aluminum foil. Continue baking until crust is golden and filling is bubbling, about 30 minutes. Let cool 10 minutes before serving.

MAKE IT CLASSIC
Prefer a more traditional
chicken potpie? Just
omit the curry powder.

Poached Cod with Tomatoes

ACTIVE TIME 25 MINUTES · TOTAL TIME 35 MINUTES

Simmer up a broth with fresh vegetables and basil for poaching tender cod fillets. Ladle everything into bowls—and serve with a fork and a spoon to enjoy every last flavorful, healthy bit. SERVES 4

- 3 cups low-sodium chicken broth
- ½ medium red onion, very thinly sliced
- 2 cups cherry tomatoes, cut in half lengthwise
- ½ pound small potatoes, preferably fingerling and purple, sliced into ¼-inch rounds
- 3 sprigs basil, plus leaves for garnish

- ¼ teaspoon red-pepper flakes
  Coarse salt and freshly ground pepper
- 4 skinless cod fillets (4 ounces each)
- 4 ounces snap peas, trimmed and thinly sliced on the bias
- 1 teaspoon fresh lemon juice, plus 4 lemon wedges, for serving
  Extra-virgin olive oil, for drizzling

In a large sauté pan with a tight-fitting lid, bring broth, onion, 1½ cups tomatoes, potatoes, basil sprigs, red-pepper flakes, and 2 teaspoons salt to a boil over high heat. Reduce heat and simmer, uncovered, until potatoes are crisp-tender, 6 to 8 minutes. Season cod with salt and pepper, add to broth mixture, and cover. Simmer until fish is opaque throughout and just cooked through, about 7 minutes.

Remove and discard basil sprigs. Add peas, remaining ½ cup tomatoes, and lemon juice to skillet, gently stirring to combine; cook just until warmed through. Divide fish, vegetables, and broth among 4 bowls. Garnish with basil leaves, drizzle with oil, and serve with lemon wedges.

Chicken with Sautéed Mushrooms

ACTIVE TIME 25 MINUTES • TOTAL TIME 25 MINUTES

This dish relies on a classic French preparation: Dredge a thin cut of meat with flour, sauté it, add vegetables, and finish by making a pan sauce with wine and broth. Voilà, dinner is served! SERVES 4

¼ cup all-purpose flour

1½ pounds chicken cutlets

Coarse salt and freshly ground pepper

1 tablespoon extra-virgin olive oil

3 tablespoons unsalted butter

2 tablespoons fresh thyme leaves, chopped

1 pound button mushrooms, trimmed and quartered

¼ cup dry white wine

¼ cup low-sodium chicken broth

¼ cup chopped fresh flat-leaf parsley leaves

Place flour in a shallow dish. Season chicken with salt and pepper, then dredge in flour, shaking off excess.

In a large skillet, heat oil and 1 tablespoon butter over medium-high. Working in batches, cook chicken until browned and cooked through, about 3 minutes per side. Transfer to a plate and tent loosely with aluminum foil to keep warm.

Reduce heat to medium, add thyme, mushrooms, and remaining 2 tablespoons butter, and cook until softened, 6 minutes. Add wine and broth, and cook, stirring, until reduced by half, 3 minutes. Season with salt and pepper. Return chicken to pan along with any accumulated juices. Top with chopped parsley before serving.

ABOUT CHICKEN CUTLETS
You can buy thin-cut chicken breasts, but you'll save money if you start with less-expensive boneless breasts and create the cutlets yourself: Slice them horizontally, place between parchment, and use a mallet to pound them evenly thin (about a quarter inch thick).

SHREDDING FRESH MOZZARELLA
This cheese lends its signature taste and texture to lasagna, but it's so soft that grating it can be tricky. The solution: Pop it in the freezer for about twenty minutes to firm it up (but not freeze it solid) before you grate.

Three-Cheese Lasagna

ACTIVE TIME 30 MINUTES • TOTAL TIME 1 HOUR

Try this smart shortcut: Make your own marinara sauce and assemble lasagna right in the same pan. Breaking the noodles into pieces allows you to get a good fit when arranging them. SERVES 4 TO 6

- 2 cans (one 28 ounces and one 15 ounces) whole peeled plum tomatoes
- 3 garlic cloves, finely chopped
- 3 tablespoons extra-virgin olive oil
  Coarse salt and freshly ground pepper
- 1 large egg yolk

- 1½ cups part-skim ricotta cheese (12 ounces), room temperature
- 1 box (12 ounces) no-boil lasagna noodles
- 2 cups shredded fresh mozzarella cheese (½ pound)
- ¼ cup grated Pecorino Romano or Parmigiano-Reggiano cheese (1 ounce)

Preheat oven to 400°F. In a food processor, pulse tomatoes (with their liquid) until coarsely pureed. In a large sauté pan, bring tomatoes, garlic, and oil to a boil over medium-high heat. Season with salt and pepper. Reduce to medium and simmer until thickened, about 12 minutes (you should have about 5 cups marinara sauce).

Meanwhile, in a bowl, mix together egg yolk, ricotta, and ½ teaspoon each salt and pepper.

Carefully pour sauce into a heatproof bowl, and return ¾ cup to pan; spread sauce evenly. Add a single layer of noodles, breaking them up to fit. Top with half the ricotta mixture, spreading evenly. Follow with a second layer of noodles, then 1½ cups marinara. Add a third layer of noodles, then remaining ricotta mixture. Follow with a final noodle layer, then remaining sauce. Sprinkle mozzarella and Pecorino over top.

Bake lasagna until golden and bubbling, 30 to 35 minutes. Let stand 10 minutes before serving.

Spicy Zucchini Frittata

ACTIVE TIME 20 MINUTES · TOTAL TIME 25 MINUTES

Corn and jalapeño bring a Southwestern spin to Italian frittata. Serve it hot or cold, for breakfast, lunch, or dinner. When corn is in season, slice it from the cob. Frozen works well, too. SERVES 4

- 2 tablespoons extra-virgin olive oil
- ½ small red onion, thinly sliced
- 1 jalapeño, thinly sliced
- 1 zucchini, thinly sliced
- 1 cup corn kernels
- Coarse salt
- 8 large eggs

Heat broiler. In a medium, heavy ovenproof skillet, heat oil over medium. Add onion and jalapeño; cook, stirring, until tender, about 5 minutes. Add zucchini and corn; cook until tender, about 7 minutes more. Season with salt.

In a bowl, whisk eggs with ½ teaspoon salt. Pour eggs into skillet with vegetables. Cook until sides just begin to set, 2 to 3 minutes.

Transfer skillet to oven, and broil until just set in the middle and lightly golden and puffed on top, 2 to 3 minutes. Serve hot or cold.

Slow Cooker

Dinner that cooks itself? With a slow cooker, this dream becomes a reality: Combine ingredients in the machine, push a button, and enjoy a hearty, homey supper hours later.

The Basics

The slow cooker (commonly referred to as Crock-Pot, which is a brand name) is an electric appliance with a ceramic, porcelain, or metal insert and a tight-fitting lid. The vessel can safely be left unattended as it cooks ingredients in liquid at low temperatures (approximately 200 degrees). Over a period of about four to eight hours, it transforms tougher cuts of meat, such as beef brisket or lamb shanks, making them wonderfully tender. The lid prevents evaporation, for great soups and saucy stews. No fuss, no stirring—you set it up in the morning and come home to a delicious dinner.

So what's the catch? Some slow-cooker recipes trade flavor for convenience. When you toss everything into the pot and walk away, you're skipping what's often the first step for a soup or stew: browning the meat, which creates a flavor base for the dish and, especially for chicken, helps keep the meat from drying out. For the recipes in this book, we've primarily developed dishes that don't require browning. For our chicken dishes, we used a slow cooker with a special metal insert that can be used for browning; if you don't have this type of appliance, just remove the skin of the chicken before cooking.

Cooking Tips

- Start with the right ingredients. Chicken breasts and lean, tender cuts of beef, pork, and lamb can dry out. Ground meat and seafood both cook too quickly for the slow cooker.

- Pay attention to the size of the slow cooker called for in a recipe. When cooking, the pot should be between halfway and two-thirds full. If it's not full enough, food can overcook. If it's too full, the machine can overflow as the food simmers and condensation accumulates.

- Resist the temptation to peek into the pot. It takes a while for a slow cooker to warm up; if you lift the lid, you release the steam and lower the temperature inside. For each time you do that, add about 15 minutes to your cooking time.

- Need even more time than a recipe calls for? Set up your ingredients in the crock, cover, and refrigerate overnight. Starting with a chilled crock and ingredients will add about an hour to your cooking time.

- Get to know your slow cooker. Different models heat at different rates and to different temperatures. If you notice that your food tends to overcook or takes longer than a recipe indicates, start adjusting the cooking time on recipes you make.

- Never put frozen food into a slow cooker; the meat may end up at an unsafe temperature for too long, causing harmful bacteria to grow.

A NOTE ABOUT SIZE

A five- to six-quart slow cooker will work for most recipes and feed four to eight people. Oval- or rectangular-shaped ones fit roasts and whole chickens more easily than round ones.

BROWNING INSERT

Some models (including this one) have a metal insert that can be used on the stovetop before being transferred to the slow cooker, or can heat up enough to brown. We like these models, as they allow you to sauté onions and other aromatics and to brown meat.

SMART SETTINGS

For slow-cooking, you just need "low" and "high" modes. But many models come with other features, such as a "keep warm" mode and a programmable timer. Decide which ones, if any, will be useful for you.

TO-GO OPTIONS

If you like taking your slow cooker to potlucks, look for features such as a locking lid and carrying case.

Spiced Chicken Stew with Carrots

ACTIVE TIME 10 MINUTES · TOTAL TIME 4 HOURS 10 MINUTES

We use a slow cooker with a browning option to crisp the chicken skin for this Moroccan-flavored dish. The stew is great on its own, but couscous would be an easy and fitting side dish. SERVES 4

- 8 bone-in chicken thighs (about 2½ pounds total)
  Coarse salt and freshly ground pepper
- 2 tablespoons olive oil (optional)
- 2 pounds carrots, cut into 1½-inch lengths
- 1 garlic clove, thinly sliced

- 1 cinnamon stick
- ½ teaspoon ground cumin
- ¼ cup golden raisins
- ½ cup fresh cilantro leaves
- ¼ cup sliced almonds, toasted (optional)

Season chicken with salt and pepper. In a 5- to 6-quart slow cooker with a browning option, brown chicken in oil; transfer to a plate. (If your slow cooker doesn't have a browning option, just remove skin from the chicken.) Add carrots, garlic, cinnamon stick, and cumin to pot. Place chicken on top. Cover and cook on high until chicken is cooked through, 4 hours (or 8 hours on low), adding raisins 15 minutes before done.

Using a slotted spoon, transfer chicken and carrots to a serving dish (remove cinnamon stick); top with cilantro and almonds. Season cooking liquid with salt and pepper. Spoon over chicken before serving.

Pulled Pork

ACTIVE TIME 10 MINUTES · TOTAL TIME 6 HOURS 30 MINUTES

Barbecue purists may claim that pulled pork has to be smoked in a pit to be the real thing, and we won't quibble with that. But this recipe, prepared right in your kitchen (on the counter, no less), is one deliciously simple variation on the theme. SERVES 8

- 1 medium onion, finely chopped
- 1 teaspoon dried oregano
- 2 dried bay leaves
- 1 chipotle in adobo sauce, minced, plus 1 tablespoon adobo
- 1 can (28 ounces) crushed tomatoes
- 1 can (14.5 ounces) whole tomatoes in puree
- 2 teaspoons coarse salt
- ½ teaspoon freshly ground pepper
- 2¾ pounds boneless pork shoulder, trimmed and halved crosswise
- 8 sandwich rolls, split, for serving
- Coleslaw, for serving
- Pickles, for serving

In a 5- to 6-quart slow cooker, combine onion, oregano, bay leaves, chipotle, adobo sauce, tomatoes (and puree), salt, and pepper. Add pork and turn to coat completely.

Cover and cook on high until meat is pull-apart tender, about 6 hours. Transfer pork to a bowl; shred with two forks. Return pork to pot, and toss with sauce. Discard bay leaves.

Serve pulled pork with rolls, coleslaw, and pickles.

Corned Beef and Cabbage

ACTIVE TIME 15 MINUTES • TOTAL TIME 5 HOURS 15 MINUTES

This celebrated Saint Patrick's Day meal is too satisfying to make only once a year. Its name comes from the process of salting—or "corning"—a large cut of beef to preserve it. SERVES 6

- 3 carrots, cut into 3-inch pieces
- 2 celery stalks, cut into 3-inch pieces
- 1 small yellow onion, cut into 1-inch wedges (root end left intact)
- ½ pound new potatoes, scrubbed and halved
- 6 sprigs thyme

- 1 corned beef brisket (about 3 pounds), plus pickling spice packet or 1 tablespoon pickling spice
- 6 cups water
- ½ head Savoy cabbage, cut into 1½-inch wedges
- Grainy mustard, for serving

In a 5- to 6-quart slow cooker, combine carrots, celery, onion, potatoes, and thyme. Place corned beef, fat side up, on top of vegetables; sprinkle with pickling spice. Pour in the water (or enough to almost cover meat). Cover and cook on high until corned beef is tender, 4 hours 15 minutes (or 8 hours 30 minutes on low). Arrange cabbage over corned beef, cover, and continue cooking until cabbage is tender, 45 minutes (or 1 hour 30 minutes on low).

Thinly slice corned beef against the grain. Drizzle beef and vegetables with cooking liquid, and serve with mustard.

EVEN BETTER THE SECOND TIME
If you have corned beef left over, make a quick hash. Fry up some of the boiled potatoes with onions and chopped corned beef; add some chopped leftover cabbage, too.

Spicy Turkey Chili

ACTIVE TIME 15 MINUTES · TOTAL TIME 3 HOURS 45 MINUTES

Think of this as a three-chile chili: It gets its depth, smokiness, and heat from serrano peppers, canned chipotles in adobo sauce, and chili powder. The heat of fresh chiles varies widely. Taste a tiny bit of your serrano; if it's incendiary, use just one. SERVES 6

- 1½ pounds boneless, skinless turkey thighs, cut into 1-inch pieces
- 1 medium yellow onion, finely chopped
- 3 garlic cloves, minced
- 1 to 2 serrano or jalapeño chiles, seeded and minced, plus sliced chiles, for serving
- 1 chipotle chile in adobo sauce, minced
- 1 can (28 ounces) whole peeled tomatoes, pureed

- 2 tablespoons chili powder
- Coarse salt
- 2 cans (15.5 ounces each) black beans, rinsed and drained
- 1 tablespoon white vinegar
- Sour cream and fresh cilantro, for serving

In a 5- to 6-quart slow cooker, combine turkey, onion, garlic, serrano chiles, chipotle chile, tomatoes, chili powder, and 1 teaspoon salt. Cover and cook on high until turkey is fork-tender, 3 hours (or 6 hours on low).

Add beans and cook until warmed through, about 30 minutes more. Stir in vinegar, and season with salt. Serve with sliced chiles, sour cream, and cilantro.

ABOUT CHIPOTLES IN ADOBO
Chipotles are dried, smoked jalapeño peppers. They are often sold in cans, in a tangy sauce called adobo, in the Latin section of supermarkets. Their smoky heat is great in soups and stews, but a little goes a long way—this recipe calls for just one. Freeze the rest in a resealable bag for up to three months.

Garlic Chicken with Barley

ACTIVE TIME 20 MINUTES · TOTAL TIME 2 HOURS 20 MINUTES

With hearty barley and sweet green peas, so evocative of spring, this meal straddles the seasons beautifully: It's hearty and satisfying, but full of fresh promise for the warm days to come. SERVES 4

1 whole chicken (3½ to 4 pounds), cut into 10 pieces

Coarse salt and freshly ground pepper

2 tablespoons olive oil

⅔ cup pearl barley

1½ cups low-sodium chicken broth

¼ cup white wine

1 medium yellow onion, thinly sliced

4 garlic cloves, thinly sliced

1½ cups frozen peas, thawed

2 teaspoons chopped fresh tarragon

Season chicken with salt and pepper. In a 5- to 6-quart slow cooker with a browning option, brown chicken in oil, 8 to 10 minutes; transfer to a plate. (If your slow cooker doesn't have a browning option, just remove skin from the chicken.) Add barley, broth, wine, onion, and garlic to pot. Season with salt and pepper. Place chicken on top. Cover and cook on low until chicken is cooked through, 2 hours.

Stir peas and tarragon into barley; season with salt and pepper; and transfer to a platter. Arrange chicken on barley and serve.

THE RIGHT WINE
A good rule of thumb is to cook with a wine you'd like to drink. A dry Sauvignon Blanc works here and would make a crisp accompaniment to the meal as well. For an alcohol-free version, substitute low-sodium chicken broth.

One Pot, Four Ways
Pot Roast

ACTIVE TIME 15 MINUTES · TOTAL TIME 5 HOURS 15 MINUTES

For pot roast—a tough cut of beef braised until succulent and tender—we start with a well-marbled chuck. Pair it with familiar carrots and potatoes, or try one of the variations that follow. SERVES 6

Classic Pot Roast

- 1 tablespoon plus 1 teaspoon cornstarch
- ¾ cup low-sodium chicken broth
- 3 tablespoons tomato paste
- 1 pound small Yukon Gold potatoes, scrubbed and halved
- 2 large carrots, cut into 2-inch pieces
- 1 medium yellow onion, cut into ½-inch wedges
- 2 tablespoons Worcestershire sauce
  Coarse salt and freshly ground pepper
- 1 beef roast (3 pounds), preferably chuck, trimmed of excess fat
- 4 garlic cloves, mashed to a paste

1. In a 5- to 6-quart slow cooker, stir together cornstarch and 2 tablespoons broth until smooth. Add remaining broth, tomato paste, potatoes, carrots, onion, and Worcestershire. Season with salt and pepper and toss.

2. Season roast with 1 teaspoon salt and ½ teaspoon pepper, and rub with garlic. Place on top of vegetables. Cover and cook on high until roast is fork-tender, 5 hours (or 8 hours on low).

3. Transfer roast to a cutting board; thinly slice against the grain. Place vegetables in a serving dish; skim fat from pan juices, then pour through a fine-mesh sieve, if desired. Serve roast and vegetables drizzled with juices.

with Broccoli Rabe and Lemon

- In step 1, omit tomato paste, carrots, and Worcestershire sauce. Add 2 sprigs **rosemary.**

- In step 2, during the last 20 minutes of cooking, add 12 ounces **broccoli rabe** to slow cooker, pressing down into juices; cook 20 minutes, then transfer to serving dish. Stir 1 teaspoon finely grated **lemon zest** plus 1 tablespoon fresh **lemon juice** into juices.

with Shiitake Mushrooms and Ginger

- In step 1, replace tomato paste with reduced-sodium **soy sauce.** Replace potatoes with **turnips,** peeled and cut into 1-inch wedges. Replace carrots with 8 ounces **shiitake mushrooms,** stemmed and sliced. Replace onion with ¼ cup minced peeled fresh **ginger.** Replace Worcestershire sauce with **hoisin sauce.**

- In step 3, garnish with sliced **scallions.**

with Sweet Potatoes and Prunes

- In step 1, omit tomato paste. Replace potatoes with **sweet potatoes,** cut into 1-inch wedges. Replace carrots with ½ cup halved **prunes.** Replace Worcestershire sauce with ¼ cup **red wine.**

- In step 3, stir an additional ½ cup halved **prunes** into sauce.

**CLASSIC
POT ROAST**
PAGE 112

POT ROAST
with Broccoli Rabe
and Lemon
PAGE 113

POT ROAST
with Shiitake
Mushrooms and Ginger
PAGE 113

POT ROAST
with Sweet Potatoes
and Prunes
PAGE 113

Potato and Bacon Soup

ACTIVE TIME 20 MINUTES · TOTAL TIME 4 HOURS 20 MINUTES

When nightfall comes early and you just can't shake the chill, this soup is exactly what you need. It's stocked with thick-cut bacon and nutritious root vegetables. Golden Gruyère toasts floating on top make the whole thing even more cozy and comforting. SERVES 8

- 1 (1-inch-thick) slab bacon (4 ounces), rind removed, cut into 1-inch pieces
- 1 pound small Yukon Gold potatoes, scrubbed and halved
- 2 leeks (white and light-green parts only), sliced into rounds and rinsed well
- 1 medium fennel bulb, chopped into ½-inch pieces, fronds reserved
- ¼ head Savoy cabbage, chopped into 1-inch pieces

- 3 garlic cloves, coarsely chopped
- 1 tablespoon plus 1 teaspoon coarsely chopped fresh thyme leaves

  Coarse salt and freshly ground pepper
- 4 cups low-sodium chicken broth
- 6 cups water

  Toasted baguette slices topped with melted cheese, such as Gruyère, Comté, or Tomme de Savoie, for serving (optional)

In a 5- to 6-quart slow cooker, place bacon and potatoes. Toss together leeks, chopped fennel, cabbage, garlic, thyme, and 2 teaspoons salt in a bowl; add to slow cooker. Pour in broth and the water (or enough water until vegetables are just covered, pressing them down to submerge).

Cover and cook on high until vegetables are tender, 4 hours (or 8 hours on low). Season with salt and pepper. Stir in reserved fennel fronds. Serve with toasted baguette slices, if desired.

Lamb Shanks and Potatoes

ACTIVE TIME 20 MINUTES · TOTAL TIME 5 HOURS 20 MINUTES

Fragrant spices and the sweetness of apricot jam are the perfect complements to rich, meaty lamb shanks. Have your butcher cut the shanks into pieces for a better fit in the slow cooker. SERVES 6

- 1 can (15 ounces) crushed tomatoes
- 3 tablespoons tomato paste
- 2 tablespoons apricot jam
- 6 garlic cloves, thinly sliced
- 3 strips orange zest
- ¾ teaspoon crushed dried rosemary
- ½ teaspoon ground ginger
- ½ teaspoon ground cinnamon
- Coarse salt and freshly ground pepper
- 3½ pounds lamb shanks, trimmed of excess fat, cut into thirds widthwise
- 1¼ pounds new potatoes, scrubbed and halved
- Fresh flat-leaf parsley leaves, for garnish

In a 5- to 6-quart slow cooker, stir together tomatoes, tomato paste, apricot jam, garlic, orange zest, rosemary, ginger, and cinnamon. Season with salt and pepper. Add lamb and potatoes, stirring to combine.

Cover and cook on high until lamb and potatoes are tender, 5 hours (or 8 hours on low). Season with salt and pepper. Serve topped with parsley.

Whole Poached Chicken with Asian Flavors

ACTIVE TIME 15 MINUTES · TOTAL TIME 2 HOURS 15 MINUTES

This light, delicate chicken isn't your typical slow-cooker dinner. But the appliance's low temperature poaches the bird beautifully, yielding moist meat in a delectable broth. SERVES 4

---

3 bunches whole scallions

1 bunch cilantro (stems and leaves)

1 whole chicken (about 4 pounds)

2 celery stalks, chopped into 2-inch pieces

12 shiitake mushrooms, stemmed

6 (¼-inch) slices peeled fresh ginger

6 star anise

2 teaspoons peppercorns, preferably white

1 tablespoon plus 2 teaspoons coarse salt

8 cups water

In a 5- to 6-quart slow cooker, place 2 bunches scallions and half a bunch of cilantro. Place the chicken on top. Add celery, mushrooms, ginger, star anise, peppercorns, and salt, arranging everything around the chicken. Add the water. Cover and cook on high until chicken is cooked through and reaches 165°F on an instant-read thermometer, 2 hours (or 4 hours on low).

Transfer chicken to a cutting board, and carve into portions; slice breast. Divide among large bowls. Use a slotted spoon to transfer mushrooms to bowls. Ladle broth over chicken and mushrooms, avoiding star anise and other ingredients (or strain first). Coarsely chop remaining cilantro and scallions, and sprinkle over each bowl before serving. (Strain remaining chicken broth, and reserve for another use.)

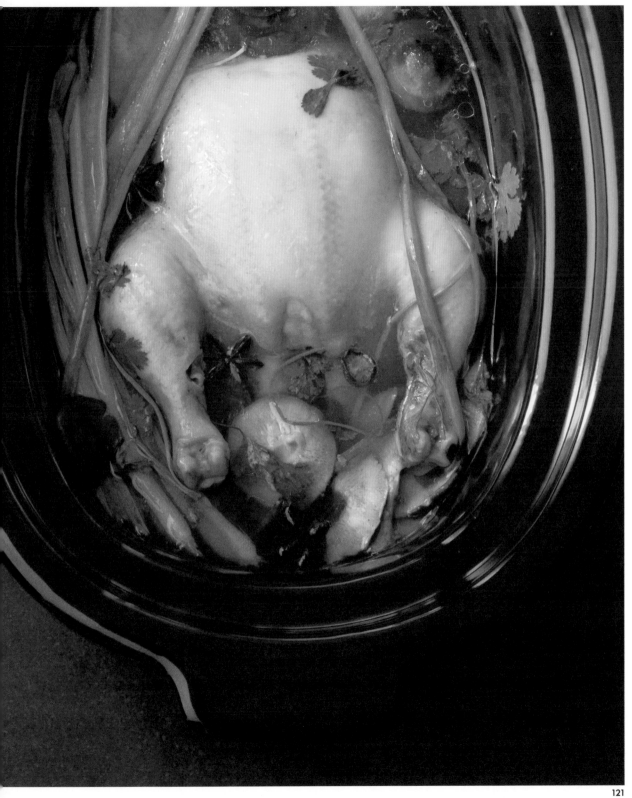

Turkey Stew with Lima Beans

ACTIVE TIME 15 MINUTES · TOTAL TIME 6 HOURS 20 MINUTES, PLUS SOAKING

The two main ingredients here aren't a common combination, but they work together beautifully. Strips of lemon zest and a squeeze of juice at the table add a little zing. SERVES 8

- 2 cups dried large lima beans (10 ounces), sorted and rinsed
- 2 boneless, skinless turkey thighs (1½ pounds total), cut into 1½-inch pieces
- Coarse salt and freshly ground pepper
- 1 tablespoon vegetable oil
- 1 large white onion, diced
- 3 garlic cloves, smashed
- ¼ cup dry white wine, such as Sauvignon Blanc
- 1½ cups low-sodium chicken broth
- 5 large strips of lemon zest; plus 2 tablespoons fresh lemon juice; and wedges, for serving

Cover beans with cold water; let sit overnight. Drain beans. Season turkey with salt and pepper.

If using a 5- to 6-quart slow cooker with a browning option: Brown turkey in oil, about 8 minutes. Transfer to a plate. Add onion and garlic; cook, stirring occasionally, until onion is translucent, 4 minutes. Add wine; bring to a boil, stirring and scraping up browned bits with a wooden spoon. Add broth, lemon zest, the beans, and the turkey to slow cooker. Season with salt and pepper.

If using a 5- to 6-quart slow cooker without a browning option: Place beans in the slow cooker. Add all other ingredients, except lemon juice and wedges.

Cover and cook on high 6 hours. (Beans should be tender and turkey will be just beginning to fall apart.) Add lemon juice and stir. Serve with lemon wedges.

Roasting Pan & Baking Dish

A roasting pan lets you cook a main course and side dishes together. A baking dish is perfect for layering ingredients to create modern takes on the classic casserole. The best part? Either way, your oven does most of the work.

The Basics

Roasting pans and baking dishes, and the techniques you use to cook with them, are similar but not identical.

ROASTING means cooking ingredients—usually meat or vegetables—in the oven in a metal pan, uncovered, at a relatively high temperature. The result: food that's browned and crisp on the outside and moist on the inside. Roasting concentrates the flavor of foods, so you don't need much more than oil and simple seasonings to enhance the dish. When a recipe calls for roasting, use a roasting pan or rimmed baking sheet.

BAKING is a term generally used for bread and pastries, but it can also refer to cooking casseroles and lasagna-style dishes with layers of ingredients. The food may be covered for part of the time, and the temperature is lower than with roasting. Use a glass or ceramic baking dish.

Cooking Tips

• For roasting, don't crowd the pan. Leave room between ingredients, or they'll steam—that means no brown, crisp edges. As they roast, turn foods occasionally with a spatula or tongs, so they brown on all sides.

• Cut vegetables in same-size pieces so they cook evenly.

• Bring roasts to room temperature before cooking. Let them sit out for about an hour (depending on the size of the roast and the temperature of the room) before putting them into the oven.

• Use an instant-read thermometer to test doneness of meat.

• Roasts benefit from resting—that is, standing at room temperature for ten to twenty minutes once they're out of the oven. This allows for carryover cooking and lets the juices redistribute throughout the meat before carving or slicing.

ROASTING PAN

Look for a pan that's twelve by sixteen inches or larger, with three-inch sides. This will fit a medium-size roast plus vegetable sides (or a large holiday roast) and will catch pan drippings. Heavyweight pans won't buckle in high heat and will allow for even browning. A pan that goes on the stovetop is a plus for making gravy. Stand-up handles are easiest to grasp and hold, while riveted handles are sturdiest.

RIMMED BAKING SHEET

You'll find these by the dozen in restaurant kitchens, but we rely on them at home, too. The large size (thirteen by eighteen inches, known as a half-sheet pan) is big enough for dinner. The low sides allow for superior browning and get bonus points for making the pan easier to clean and store than a roasting pan. Look for thicker pans, which won't buckle.

BAKING DISH

The most common and useful sizes are nine by thirteen inches and eight-inch square; the former is often referred to as a lasagna pan. Ceramic and glass perform similarly. These dishes are meant to go from oven to table, so choose one with an appearance you like.

Lamb with Asparagus and Potatoes

ACTIVE TIME 35 MINUTES · TOTAL TIME 3 HOURS

Here's a meal elegant enough for any special occasion—but don't wait for one to try it. Yukon Golds are the best spuds to use because they hold their shape as they roast. SERVES 8

Zest (removed in wide strips and chopped) and juice from 2 lemons

1 head garlic, cloves smashed

2 tablespoons chopped fresh rosemary

½ cup extra-virgin olive oil

1 boneless leg of lamb roast (about 4 pounds), tied at 1-inch intervals

Coarse salt and freshly ground pepper

2 pounds small Yukon Gold potatoes, peeled

1 bunch asparagus, trimmed

In a bowl, combine lemon zest and juice, garlic, and rosemary; whisk in ¼ cup plus 2 tablespoons oil. Season lamb with salt and pepper. Place in a large resealable bag, and add marinade. Seal bag, pressing to remove as much air as possible. Turn bag several times to coat lamb in marinade. Let sit at room temperature 1 hour (or refrigerate overnight), flipping bag halfway through.

Preheat oven to 450°F. (If lamb was marinated overnight, remove from refrigerator 1 hour before cooking.) Toss potatoes with remaining 2 tablespoons oil, and season with salt and pepper. Transfer to a roasting pan, and roast 20 minutes.

Remove lamb from marinade, and season with salt and pepper. Push potatoes to edges of pan, add marinade and lamb, and roast 15 minutes. Reduce oven temperature to 300°F, and cook 40 minutes. Add asparagus, tossing to coat in pan juices, and cook until lamb is medium-rare (an instant-read thermometer should read 130°F when inserted in thickest part of lamb), about 20 minutes more.

Tent lamb with foil, and let rest 20 minutes before carving and serving. If necessary to fully cook vegetables, return them to oven while meat is resting.

  ROASTING PAN & BAKING DISH

Broiled Striped Bass with Tomatoes

ACTIVE TIME 15 MINUTES • TOTAL TIME 30 MINUTES

When you're looking for a fast, no-fuss dinner, turn on the broiler. This technique is similar to grilling, but the heat comes from above instead of below, and you can broil in any weather. SERVES 4

1½ pounds skinless striped-bass fillet

2 teaspoons grated garlic

1 teaspoon dried oregano

2 teaspoons finely grated lemon zest, plus 1 tablespoon fresh lemon juice

Coarse salt and freshly ground pepper

3 tablespoons extra-virgin olive oil

1 large bulb fennel, thinly sliced lengthwise, with stalks and ¼ cup fronds reserved

1 pint cherry or grape tomatoes

½ cup brine-cured black olives, such as Kalamata

Heat broiler, with rack about 8 inches from heating element. Make diagonal slashes ¼ inch deep at 2-inch intervals across top of fish. Stir together garlic, oregano, lemon zest and juice, 1 teaspoon salt, ¼ teaspoon pepper, and 2 tablespoons oil; spread on both sides of fish, rubbing into slashes. Place fennel stalks lengthwise on a rimmed baking sheet. Top with fish, slashed side up.

Toss fennel slices with tomatoes, olives, remaining tablespoon oil, ½ teaspoon salt, and ¼ teaspoon pepper; spread evenly around fish. Broil until fish is just cooked and opaque throughout and vegetables are charred in places, 8 to 10 minutes. (If the vegetables begin to blacken, tent with foil.) Divide fish and vegetables among 4 plates; garnish with fennel fronds.

Pork Chops with Bacon and Cabbage

ACTIVE TIME 40 MINUTES · TOTAL TIME 40 MINUTES

A popular Italian recipe—pork roast braised in milk—inspired this simple version, with chops and vegetables cooked right in the same pan. Consider it your new favorite comfort food. SERVES 4

- 2 tablespoons extra-virgin olive oil
- 4 bone-in pork chops (1 inch thick)
  Coarse salt and freshly ground pepper
- 4 strips bacon, coarsely chopped
- 1 yellow onion, cut into ½-inch slices
- 1 head green cabbage (about 2½ pounds), cored and cut into 8 wedges
- 3 tablespoons all-purpose flour
- 3 cups whole milk

Preheat oven to 400°F. In a large roasting pan set across two burners, heat oil over high. Season pork with salt and pepper; add to pan and cook until browned on one side, 3 to 5 minutes. Flip and cook 1 minute more. Transfer to a plate.

Reduce heat to medium. Add bacon and cook until golden, about 5 minutes. Add onion and cook until softened, 5 minutes. Add cabbage, cut-side down, and cook until light golden, about 6 minutes. Flip and cook until slightly tender, about 3 minutes. Add flour and stir until coated. Add milk and cook, stirring constantly, until thickened, about 4 minutes. Season with salt and pepper, then nestle pork chops in sauce. Transfer pan to oven. Bake until pork is cooked through, about 10 minutes.

SHOPPING FOR CHOPS
Pork is a lot safer, as well as leaner, than it was a generation ago. That's good news—but less fat also means it's easier for the meat to dry out as it cooks. Look for thick bone-in chops, which are more likely to stay moist, and take care not to overcook them.

VARIATIONS ON THE THEME
You can add paprika and minced garlic with the salt, or use sliced potatoes instead of bread.

Spatchcocked Chicken with Herbs and Lemon

ACTIVE TIME 25 MINUTES · TOTAL TIME 1 HOUR

This funny-sounding technique yields seriously good results. Spatchcocking (flattening) a whole chicken helps it cook evenly— in about 30 minutes! Bread rounds out the meal. SERVES 4 TO 6

- 1 whole chicken (3½ to 4 pounds)
- 3 tablespoons unsalted butter, room temperature
- 1½ teaspoons chunky sea salt, such as Maldon
- 8 slices rustic bread (from about ½ loaf), ¾ inch thick
- 1 cup fresh Thai or regular basil leaves
- 1 cup fresh mint leaves
- 1 lemon, halved

Preheat oven to 425°F. Place chicken, breast side down, on a work surface. Starting at thigh end, cut along 1 side of backbone with kitchen shears. Turn chicken around, and cut along other side. (Discard or save backbone for stock.) Flip chicken over and press firmly on breastbone to flatten. Rub with 2 tablespoons butter, and season with salt.

Dividing evenly, spread remaining tablespoon butter on 1 side of bread slices. Place side by side, buttered side up, on a parchment-lined rimmed baking sheet, and lay chicken on top. Roast until chicken is golden brown and a thermometer inserted into thickest part of breast (do not touch bone) reaches 160°F, 30 to 35 minutes.

Remove chicken from oven; let rest on baking sheet 10 minutes. Scatter with herbs; squeeze lemon juice over chicken. Cut chicken and bread into serving pieces; place on a platter. Pour pan juices over chicken and serve.

Salmon with Cabbage and Kale

ACTIVE TIME 10 MINUTES • TOTAL TIME 25 MINUTES

You may not think to roast leafy greens, but high heat works magic on them, intensifying their flavor. Cook salmon alongside the greens, and finish everything with a lemony vinaigrette. SERVES 4

- 1 bunch Tuscan kale, tough stems and ribs removed, leaves thinly sliced
- ½ head Savoy cabbage, cored and sliced
- ¼ cup plus 2 tablespoons olive oil

  Coarse salt and freshly ground pepper

- 4 skinless salmon fillets (4 to 6 ounces each)
- 1 teaspoon finely grated lemon zest, plus 2 tablespoons fresh lemon juice
- ¼ cup fresh dill, chopped
- 1 teaspoon Dijon mustard

Preheat oven to 450°F. On a rimmed baking sheet, toss kale and cabbage with 2 tablespoons oil, season with salt and pepper, and arrange in an even layer; bake 6 minutes. Stir. Season salmon with salt and pepper, and nestle among the greens. Bake until salmon is cooked through, about 10 minutes.

Meanwhile, whisk together lemon zest and juice, dill, mustard, and remaining ¼ cup oil. Season with salt and pepper. Serve salmon and vegetables drizzled with dressing.

Provençal Vegetable Tian

ACTIVE TIME 20 MINUTES • TOTAL TIME 1 HOUR 25 MINUTES

Showcase the best of the summer garden with this meatless main course. All you do is slice and stack; the vegetables' flavors meld as they cook. Crusty bread is an essential accompaniment. SERVES 8

- 6 tablespoons extra-virgin olive oil
- 1 large leek (white and light-green parts only), thinly sliced and rinsed well
- 1 Yukon Gold potato, sliced ¼ inch thick
  Coarse salt and freshly ground pepper
- 1 small eggplant, trimmed and sliced ¼ inch thick

- 1 large zucchini (8 ounces), sliced ¼ inch thick
- 3 large beefsteak tomatoes, sliced ¼ inch thick
- ¼ cup brine-cured black olives, such as Kalamata, roughly chopped
- 2 teaspoons fresh thyme leaves, plus 3 sprigs

Preheat oven to 450°F. Drizzle 1 tablespoon oil in a 9-by-13-inch baking dish. Layer half the leek slices in dish, then cover with half the potato; season with ½ teaspoon salt and a pinch of pepper. Then layer with half the eggplant, half the zucchini, and half the tomatoes; season with ½ teaspoon salt and a pinch of pepper. Scatter with half the olives and half the thyme. Drizzle with 2 tablespoons oil. Repeat layering and seasoning with remaining vegetables. Drizzle with remaining 3 tablespoons oil, add thyme sprigs, and cover loosely with aluminum foil.

Bake 20 minutes, then remove foil. Press vegetables down with a spatula, and bake until potato is tender and edges are well caramelized, about 45 minutes more. Let cool 10 minutes before serving.

Roast Beef with Acorn Squash

ACTIVE TIME 15 MINUTES · TOTAL TIME 1 HOUR 15 MINUTES

Beef tenderloin is coated with a compound (or flavored) butter—
a tasty trick that works for meat, fish, and vegetables. Keep this
recipe in mind for holidays or Sunday dinners. SERVES 6 TO 8

- 1 beef tenderloin (3½ pounds), tied with kitchen twine at 2-inch intervals
  Coarse salt and freshly ground pepper
- 4 tablespoons unsalted butter, room temperature
- 3 tablespoons grainy mustard
- 1 tablespoon Dijon mustard

- 2 small acorn squash, seeded and cut into 1-inch wedges
- 1 head frisée, torn (about 3 cups)
- ½ cup fresh flat-leaf parsley leaves
- 1 tablespoon sherry vinegar
- 2 tablespoons extra-virgin olive oil

Let beef stand at room temperature for 1 hour; pat dry. Preheat oven to 425°F. Season beef with salt and pepper. Stir together 3 tablespoons butter and both mustards; spread over tenderloin to cover.

Place beef on a rimmed baking sheet. Arrange squash around beef, and brush squash with remaining tablespoon butter; season with salt and pepper. Roast until an instant-read thermometer inserted into center of the beef reaches 130°F (for medium-rare) or 140°F (for medium), 30 to 40 minutes (time will vary depending on the thickness of cut), flipping squash halfway through. Let rest 15 minutes before slicing.

Toss frisée, parsley, and squash with vinegar and oil; season with salt and pepper. Serve tenderloin with greens and squash.

ROASTING PAN & BAKING DISH

One Pot, Four Ways
Roast Chicken

ACTIVE TIME 15 MINUTES · TOTAL TIME 1 HOUR 10 MINUTES

Roast chicken is so good, you may not want to stray from the classic—but then you would never know how easy it is to transform the flavor by varying the seasonings and vegetables. SERVES 4

Roast Chicken with Herb Butter

- 2 lemons
- 1½ tablespoons unsalted butter, room temperature
- 1 tablespoon finely chopped fresh flat-leaf parsley leaves
- 1 tablespoon finely chopped fresh dill

Coarse salt
- 1 whole chicken (4 to 5 pounds)
- 1¾ pounds russet potatoes, scrubbed and cut lengthwise into 1-inch wedges
- 1 tablespoon extra-virgin olive oil

1. Preheat oven to 425°F. Zest 1 lemon, then cut both into quarters. Combine zest with butter, parsley, dill, and 2 teaspoons salt. Rub butter mixture under skin of chicken. Tie legs together, and tuck wing tips beneath body. Place on a rimmed baking sheet.

2. Toss potatoes with oil; season with salt. Scatter potatoes around chicken; roast 20 minutes.

3. Flip potatoes and add lemon quarters to pan. Roast until an instant-read thermometer inserted into thickest part of a thigh reads 165°F, 25 to 35 minutes. Let rest 10 minutes before carving and serving. Return potatoes to oven and roast until golden, 10 minutes.

TIMING IS EVERYTHING
For the most even results, let chicken come to room temperature (this takes about an hour) before roasting. Once it's out of the oven, don't skip the resting time. Those ten minutes allow the juices to redistribute, for moist, tender meat.

  ROASTING PAN & BAKING DISH

with Paprika and Roasted Garlic

- In step 1, rub chicken with 1 tablespoon **olive oil**. Replace herb butter with a rub: Combine 1 tablespoon **paprika**, ½ teaspoon **dried oregano,** and 1 tablespoon **coarse salt**. Rub all over chicken.

- In step 2, replace potatoes with 2 large **carrots,** cut into 2-inch lengths, and 2 medium **sweet potatoes,** cut into ¾-inch wedges.

- In step 3, replace lemon with 1 head **garlic,** halved crosswise and tossed with 1 tablespoon **olive oil**. Tent chicken with foil to prevent overbrowning, if needed. Brush with pan juices before serving.

with Scallion, Ginger, and Lime

- In step 1, replace herb butter with a paste: In a food processor, combine 3 tablespoons vegetable **oil**, 8 chopped **scallions**, ¼ cup chopped peeled fresh **ginger,** 4 **garlic cloves,** 1 teaspoon **lime zest,** and 1 tablespoon **coarse salt;** rub half of paste under skin.

- In step 2, replace potatoes with parsnips, cut into 3-inch pieces.

- In step 3, replace lemon with 12 ounces **brussels sprouts,** halved and tossed with 1 tablespoon **vegetable oil;** season with **salt** and **pepper.** Serve with remaining paste.

with Lemon and Parsley

- In step 1, omit herb butter. Season chicken with salt. Whisk together ⅓ cup chopped fresh flat-leaf **parsley,** ½ cup extra-virgin **olive oil,** zest and juice of half a **lemon,** ½ cup grated **Parmigiano-Reggiano,** and ½ teaspoon **coarse salt**. Set aside.

- In step 2, replace russets with 1 pound **new potatoes,** scrubbed and halved.

- In step 3, replace lemon with 1 small bunch trimmed **asparagus,** tossed with 1 tablespoon **olive oil** and **salt and pepper**. After chicken rests, spoon reserved sauce over chicken and vegetables.

ROAST CHICKEN
with Herb Butter
PAGE 142

ROAST CHICKEN
with Paprika and Roasted Garlic
PAGE 143

ROAST CHICKEN
with Scallion, Ginger, and Lime
PAGE 143

ROAST CHICKEN
with Lemon and Parsley
PAGE 143

Spiced Cod with Couscous

ACTIVE TIME 15 MINUTES • TOTAL TIME 35 MINUTES

Make this once, and we're pretty sure it will become a regular at your dinner table. The method couldn't be easier: Bake cod fillets right on top of couscous. (Oh, and it tastes great, too!) SERVES 4

- 1 teaspoon ground coriander
- ½ teaspoon paprika
- ½ teaspoon ground cumin
- Coarse salt and freshly ground pepper
- 1¼ cups water
- ½ pound carrots (about 4 medium), quartered lengthwise and cut on diagonal
- 1 cup couscous
- ½ cup slivered almonds
- ½ cup raisins
- ¼ cup chopped fresh mint leaves, plus sprigs for garnish
- 1 tablespoon olive oil
- 4 skinless cod fillets (6 ounces each)
- Lemon wedges, for serving

Preheat oven to 450°F. Mix together coriander, paprika, cumin, ½ teaspoon salt, and ¼ teaspoon pepper. In a 9-by-13-inch baking dish, mix together the water, carrots, couscous, almonds, raisins, mint, oil, 1 teaspoon salt, and ¼ teaspoon pepper.

Place cod on top of couscous mixture, and season with spice mixture. Cover pan with aluminum foil; bake until fish is opaque throughout, 20 minutes.

Fluff couscous with a fork. Transfer fish and couscous mixture to plates. Top with mint, and serve with lemon wedges.

GO FISH
A versatile and mild white fish, cod pairs well with just about any seasonings you want to use. You can substitute salmon fillets here; they also work beautifully with the flavors of this dish.

  **ROASTING PAN & BAKING DISH**

Sausage with Acorn Squash and Onions

ACTIVE TIME 10 MINUTES · TOTAL TIME 30 MINUTES

The English have bangers and mash (sausage and potatoes)—now here's bangers and squash. A sprinkling of sharp cheese plays off the natural sweetness of squash and dried cherries. SERVES 4

- 1 large acorn squash, halved, seeded, and cut into ½-inch slices
- 1 red onion, cut into ¼-inch wedges
- 3 tablespoons olive oil
  Coarse salt and freshly ground pepper
- 4 hot or sweet Italian sausages (¾ pound total)
- ½ cup grated Asiago cheese (2 ounces)
- 1 tablespoon chopped fresh sage leaves
- ¼ cup dried cherries, chopped

Preheat oven to 475°F. On a rimmed baking sheet, toss squash and onion with the oil and arrange in a single layer; season with salt and pepper. Add sausages to sheet. Roast until vegetables are just tender, 15 to 18 minutes.

Heat broiler, with rack about 8 inches from heating element. Sprinkle Asiago and sage over vegetables, and broil until cheese is browned and bubbling and sausages are cooked through, 3 minutes. Serve with cherries sprinkled on top.

ABOUT ACORN SQUASH
Mild, nutty acorn squash abounds in fall and early winter. Unlike some of its relatives, it has thin edible skin, so there's no need to peel it. Cut squash crosswise into slices to show off its pretty petal shape.

Mexican-Style Lasagna

ACTIVE TIME 20 MINUTES · TOTAL TIME 1 HOUR 20 MINUTES

Swap corn tortillas for noodles and salsa for tomato sauce, then add beans and a healthy dose of fresh spinach. The result? A crowd-pleasing dinner you can feel good about serving. SERVES 4

- 1 cup fresh cilantro leaves
- 4 scallions, coarsely chopped
  Coarse salt and freshly ground pepper
- 10 ounces fresh baby spinach
- 8 corn tortillas (6 inches)

- 1 can (15.5 ounces) pinto beans, rinsed and drained
- 1 cup prepared salsa (mild or medium)
- 8 ounces pepper Jack cheese, grated (about 2 cups)
  Vegetable cooking spray

Preheat oven to 425°F. In a food processor, combine cilantro, scallions, 1 teaspoon salt, and ¼ teaspoon pepper with as much spinach as will fit; pulse, adding remaining spinach in batches, just until coarsely chopped.

Coat an 8-inch square baking dish with cooking spray. Lay 4 tortillas in bottom of dish, overlapping slightly. Layer with half of the beans, salsa, spinach mixture, and pepper Jack; repeat with remaining ingredients, beginning with tortillas and ending with cheese and pressing down gently.

Cover dish with foil; place on a rimmed baking sheet. Bake until bubbling, 25 to 30 minutes; remove foil and continue baking until golden, 15 to 20 minutes more. Cool 5 to 10 minutes before serving.

MAKE IT AHEAD
You can prep and assemble this dish up to a day in advance, then cover it with foil and refrigerate. Leave it covered and pop it into the oven, following directions but adding five to ten minutes to the initial baking time.

  ROASTING PAN & BAKING DISH

Tuscan Pork Roast

ACTIVE TIME 20 MINUTES • TOTAL TIME 1 HOUR 45 MINUTES

A simple spice rub infuses every bite of this boneless pork loin. Use a meat thermometer to prevent overcooking. Leftover pork makes excellent sandwiches. SERVES 6

3 pounds boneless pork loin, tied
  Coarse salt and freshly ground pepper

2 teaspoons fennel seeds

2 teaspoons coriander seeds

1 teaspoon black peppercorns
  Extra-virgin olive oil

2 large fennel bulbs, halved through core and cut into ½-inch wedges

4 garlic cloves

8 fresh medium-hot chiles, such as Italian cherry peppers, halved or whole

1 cup mixed olives

Let pork stand at room temperature 30 minutes. Rub pork all over with 1 teaspoon salt. Coarsely grind seeds and peppercorns in a spice grinder or with a mortar and pestle; rub all over pork. Preheat oven to 425°F.

Rub pork with oil to coat generously. Place on a rimmed baking sheet, and roast until sizzling, about 15 minutes.

Reduce heat to 375°F. Toss fennel, garlic, and chiles with just enough oil to coat; season with salt and pepper. Remove pork from oven, and add vegetables to sheet, arranging in a single layer.

Baste pork and roast until center reaches 145°F on an instant-read thermometer and vegetables are tender and golden, about 30 minutes more. Add olives and roast until hot, about 5 minutes. Let pork rest 15 minutes before slicing. Toss fennel, chiles, and olives together, and serve with pork.

Stuffed Tomatoes

ACTIVE TIME 15 MINUTES · TOTAL TIME 55 MINUTES

Toss together tuna and white beans to tuck into tomatoes
(a melon baller is perfect for scooping out the seeds). A cheesy
breadcrumb topping gets irresistibly crisp in the oven. SERVES 6

- 1 cup fresh breadcrumbs
- ½ cup grated Parmigiano-Reggiano cheese
- 1 tablespoon olive oil
  Coarse salt and freshly ground pepper
- 6 medium tomatoes
- 1 can (15.5 ounces) white beans, drained and rinsed

- 1 teaspoon minced garlic
- 2 teaspoons Dijon mustard
- 2 teaspoons finely grated lemon zest, plus 1 tablespoon fresh lemon juice
- 1 can (5 ounces) light tuna in oil, drained and flaked

Preheat oven to 425°F. In a bowl, stir together ½ cup breadcrumbs, ¼ cup Parmigiano-Reggiano, and the oil; season with salt and pepper.

Remove top quarter of tomatoes, and scoop out core and seeds. Season tomato shells with salt and pepper. Chop ¼ cup of the core; discard seeds and remaining core. In a bowl, slightly mash about half the beans, then stir in chopped tomato, remaining ½ cup breadcrumbs and ¼ cup Parmigiano-Reggiano, the garlic, mustard, and lemon zest and juice. Gently fold in tuna and remaining beans. Season with salt and pepper.

Transfer tomato shells to a baking dish, and fill each with tuna mixture, dividing evenly and mounding slightly. Top with breadcrumb-cheese mixture. Loosely cover with foil, and bake until softened slightly, 30 minutes. Uncover and bake until breadcrumbs are golden brown, 5 to 10 minutes. Serve immediately.

  ROASTING PAN & BAKING DISH

TUNA TIPS

Our recipes almost always call for light tuna packed in oil. One taste should tell you why. The fish is moister and more flavorful than its white, water-packed counterpart. The oil also adds richness and helps to bind ingredients together.

Pork with Parsnips and Sweet Potatoes

ACTIVE TIME 20 MINUTES · TOTAL TIME 45 MINUTES

Pork tenderloin cooks quickly and marries well with a wide range of flavors: Here we coat it with brown sugar and cayenne, and serve it with gingery vegetables and peppery greens. SERVES 4

- 1 large sweet potato, peeled, halved, and sliced ½ inch thick
- 3 large parsnips, halved and cut into 2-inch pieces
- 1 tablespoon finely grated peeled fresh ginger
- 3 tablespoons olive oil, plus more for serving

- 2 tablespoons light-brown sugar
- ¼ teaspoon cayenne pepper
- 1 pork tenderloin (about 1 pound), excess fat and silver skin removed
- Coarse salt
- 1 bunch watercress, trimmed
- Lime wedges, for serving

Preheat oven to 475°F. On a rimmed baking sheet, toss sweet potato, parsnips, and ginger with oil and spread in an even layer. Mix together brown sugar and cayenne, and rub all over pork; add to sheet. Season pork and vegetables with salt, and roast until an instant-read thermometer inserted in center of pork reads 145°F, 20 to 22 minutes. Let pork rest 10 minutes.

Toss vegetables with watercress, drizzle with oil, and season with salt. Slice pork and serve with any accumulated juices from sheet, the salad, and lime wedges.

ABOUT PARSNIPS
This pale winter vegetable looks a lot like a carrot, and it should—the two are cousins. But unlike those crudités-platter favorites, parsnips are best cooked. They have a sweet, nutty flavor and a low calorie count and are rich in fiber.

Roasted Tilefish with Potatoes and Capers

ACTIVE TIME 15 MINUTES · TOTAL TIME 55 MINUTES

Think of this as fish and chips—minus the frying. Most of the prep is in slicing the potatoes, but a mandoline or other adjustable slicer makes quick work of the task. SERVES 4

- 2 pounds Yukon Gold potatoes, peeled
- 5 tablespoons unsalted butter, melted, plus more for pan
- Coarse salt and freshly ground pepper
- 2 garlic cloves, minced
- 3 to 4 tablespoons capers, rinsed and drained
- 2 skinless tilefish fillets (12 ounces each), or other white fish, halved crosswise
- ¼ cup chopped fresh flat-leaf parsley leaves

Preheat oven to 450°F. Slice potatoes very thin (about 1/16 inch thick) with a mandoline or sharp knife.

In a buttered 9-by-13-inch baking dish, arrange one third of potatoes, overlapping slightly. Brush with melted butter; season with salt and pepper. Scatter one third of garlic and half of the capers on top. Repeat process to make another layer. Top with remaining potatoes; brush with melted butter, and season with salt and pepper.

Cover pan with aluminum foil; roast until potatoes just begin to color, 16 to 18 minutes. Remove foil and roast until edges are pale golden, about 10 minutes more.

Meanwhile, stir together remaining garlic and melted butter in a dish. Dip fillets in mixture, season with salt and pepper, then place on top of potatoes. Roast until fillets are cooked through, about 10 minutes. Sprinkle with parsley just before serving.

Chicken with Tomatoes, Olives, and Feta

ACTIVE TIME 10 MINUTES · TOTAL TIME 1 HOUR

Take a trip to the sunny Mediterranean coast at dinnertime—tomatoes, olives and olive oil, and fresh herbs are hallmarks of the region's famed healthful cuisine. SERVES 4

- 8 bone-in chicken thighs (about 2½ pounds)
- 3 tablespoons extra-virgin olive oil
- 1 pint grape tomatoes, halved lengthwise
- ½ cup pitted Spanish olives
- 6 medium shallots, halved lengthwise
- 3 sprigs thyme
  Coarse salt and freshly ground pepper
  Crumbled feta cheese and fresh mint leaves, for serving

Preheat oven to 375°F. Combine chicken, oil, tomatoes, olives, shallots, and thyme in a bowl. Season with salt and pepper and toss. Transfer to a roasting pan, and arrange chicken mixture, skin-side up, in a single layer. Roast until a thermometer inserted into thickest parts of the thighs (do not touch bones) reaches 165°F, 35 to 40 minutes.

Transfer chicken to a platter, and tent with foil. Return vegetables to oven, and roast until golden brown in places, about 10 minutes more. Transfer vegetables (with juices) to platter with chicken, and season with salt and pepper. Top with feta and mint, and serve.

Rib Eye with Root Vegetables

ACTIVE TIME 10 MINUTES · TOTAL TIME 25 MINUTES

For a memorable dinner, consider the rib eye. It's a pricey cut, but cooking it yourself is a bargain compared to going out to a steak house. A little horseradish butter is all the finish it needs. SERVES 4 TO 6

- 1 large head celery root, peeled, halved, and cut into ¼-inch slices
- 2 large carrots, thinly sliced
- 1 tablespoon extra-virgin olive oil
- 2 boneless rib-eye steaks (1 pound each; 1¼ inches thick), excess fat trimmed

- Coarse salt and freshly ground pepper
- 1 tablespoon unsalted butter, room temperature
- 2 teaspoons prepared horseradish
- 1 teaspoon Dijon mustard
- ¼ cup snipped fresh chives

Heat broiler, with rack 8 inches from heating element. On a rimmed baking sheet, toss celery root and carrots with oil and spread in an even layer. Pat steaks dry, and add to sheet; season vegetables and steaks with salt and pepper. Broil until vegetables are tender and steaks are browned, flipping halfway through, 8 to 10 minutes. Tent steaks with foil, and let rest 10 minutes.

Meanwhile, stir together butter, horseradish, and mustard; season with salt and pepper and spread on steaks. Sprinkle with chives before serving.

ROASTING PAN & BAKING DISH

Mustard Salmon with Cabbage and Potatoes

ACTIVE TIME 10 MINUTES · TOTAL TIME 50 MINUTES

There's easy, then there's *really* easy. This recipe falls into the latter category. All you need are a few quality ingredients and minimal prep time. The only thing we didn't skimp on is flavor. SERVES 4

- 4 cups shredded red cabbage (from half a small head)
- 12 new potatoes, scrubbed and halved
- Extra-virgin olive oil
- Coarse salt and freshly ground pepper

- 2 tablespoons grainy mustard
- 2 tablespoons prepared horseradish
- Grated zest and juice of 1 lemon
- 1 pound skinless salmon fillet

Preheat oven to 400°F. In a roasting pan, toss cabbage and potatoes with olive oil; season with salt and pepper. Roast for 25 minutes.

In a bowl, combine mustard, horseradish, and lemon zest; coat salmon with mustard mixture. Nestle salmon in pan, pushing potatoes and cabbage to edges, and roast 15 minutes. Squeeze lemon juice over all and serve.

Pressure Cooker

A pressure cooker slashes cooking time, and it's easier to use than ever. In fact, this single piece of cookware could change your life—or at least your dinnertime routine. Have risotto on the table in minutes, or serve beef stew on a busy weeknight.

The Basics

A pressure cooker is a pot with a lid that seals tightly. When you bring the liquid inside to a boil, the steam can't escape, so pressure builds up and raises the temperature of the liquid, making it hotter than ordinary boiling water. At the elevated temperature, dishes cook in about a third of the time they normally need. The pressure cooker is best for dishes that usually have long cooking times: meat, beans, hearty grains, and root vegetables.

Don't be scared off by stories of pressure cookers blowing their tops. Unlike their vintage predecessors, today's models have safety mechanisms that prevent the lid from opening until the pressure has been released completely.

There are stovetop and electric (countertop) pressure cookers. With a stovetop version, you'll generally start the sealed pot off over medium-high heat to build pressure quickly. Keep an eye on the pot because it will indicate when the proper pressure for cooking has been reached, at which point you reduce the heat to maintain pressure. Electric models adjust automatically. At the end of the cooking time, release the pressure using the method appropriate for your model.

Cooking Tips

- Pressure cookers are not all the same—be sure to read your manual and follow the instructions, in terms of both cooking and releasing the pressure.

- Liquid is necessary for the pressure cooker to create steam. It doesn't have to be water; wine or broth works, too. Just don't fill the pot more than two-thirds full; some space is needed to build up pressure.

- Cut ingredients into uniform pieces so they cook evenly.

- You can brown and sauté ingredients in a stovetop pressure cooker before securing the lid—a bonus for building flavor. You can also put the pot back on the heat with the cover off once you've released the pressure; at this point, you can stir in more delicate ingredients, such as seafood and green vegetables, which would otherwise overcook in the extra-high heat.

- Food can overcook easily, so be sure to follow the recipe carefully. The cooking time begins once the pressure has been reached.

- Many models come with a rack or basket inside, so you can cook ingredients separately—say, vegetables for a side dish along with a stew.

STOVETOP OR ELECTRIC?

We prefer stovetop. The base is essentially a saucepan, so it's easy to use for sautéing and browning to develop a flavor base. Some electric models have a "browning" mode, but it may not heat up enough to be effective. The advantage of electric pressure cookers is that they adjust the heat for you, so you don't have to monitor them—however, it also means you have less control.

HOW MUCH PRESSURE?

Pressure cookers are made with several types of pressure regulators; they work differently, but all are effective. The important thing is to make sure the regulator has a maximum operating pressure of fifteen psi (pounds per square inch); if a pressure cooker does not have this high-pressure setting, cook times will be longer, throwing off the results of recipes created for that setting.

A NOTE ABOUT SIZE

The pressure cooker can't be filled past two-thirds, so it's a good idea to invest in a larger model. Six to eight quarts is a good size for serving four to eight people.

MATERIAL MATTERS

For stovetop models, the basic choice is between an aluminum and stainless-steel base. The former conducts heat well and is inexpensive, but it can be flimsy; plus, the metal can react with acidic foods. The latter costs more but is sturdy and durable.

Beef Short Ribs with Potato-Carrot Mash

ACTIVE TIME 30 MINUTES · TOTAL TIME 1 HOUR 30 MINUTES

Short ribs are a special, restaurant-worthy meal. Using the pressure cooker means you don't have to set aside an afternoon to make them. Carrots add sweetness to the classic mash. SERVES 6

- ½ cup all-purpose flour
- 6 beef short ribs (about 3¼ pounds), about 4 inches long

  Coarse salt and freshly ground pepper
- 3 tablespoons unsalted butter
- 1 small yellow onion, finely chopped
- 2 garlic cloves, minced
- 1 tablespoon fresh thyme leaves
- ¾ cup dry red wine, such as Cabernet Sauvignon or Merlot
- ¼ cup water
- 2 russet potatoes, peeled and cut into 2-inch pieces
- 4 medium carrots, cut into 2-inch pieces

Place flour in a shallow dish. Season beef with salt and pepper, then coat in flour, shaking off excess. In 6-quart pressure cooker, melt 1 tablespoon butter over medium-high. Working in batches, add beef and cook until browned on all sides, about 8 minutes; transfer to a plate.

Add onion, garlic, and thyme to pressure cooker; sauté until soft, 4 minutes. Add wine and the water; cook, stirring and scraping up browned bits with a wooden spoon, 1 minute. Return beef to pressure cooker. Fill steamer basket insert with potatoes and carrots, and place over meat.

Secure lid. Bring to high pressure over medium-high heat; reduce heat to maintain pressure and cook until meat is tender, about 50 minutes. Remove from heat, vent pressure, then remove lid. Transfer vegetables to a bowl with remaining 2 tablespoons butter and mash; season with salt and pepper. Serve short ribs with potato-carrot mash, and drizzle with cooking liquid.

ABOUT SHORT RIBS

This recipe uses English-cut short ribs: The meat is cut between the bones. You may also see flanken-style short ribs, which are cut across the bones (so each piece has several short cross-sections of bone in it). Boneless short ribs are just what the name implies: meat removed from the bone (see page 191 for a recipe using this cut).

SOAK IT UP
This dish is great with crusty bread or spooned over polenta. Precooked polenta, sold in tubes in most grocery stores, is good to have on hand: just slice, warm, and serve.

Chicken Cacciatore

ACTIVE TIME 25 MINUTES · TOTAL TIME 35 MINUTES

Whether cooked in the Italian countryside or an American kitchen, "hunter's-style" chicken—made here with tomatoes, peppers, and mushrooms—always satisfies. SERVES 4

---

8 bone-in chicken thighs (about 2½ pounds)

Coarse salt and freshly ground black pepper

2 tablespoons olive oil

12 ounces button mushrooms, trimmed and quartered

4 garlic cloves, minced

2 teaspoons chopped fresh rosemary

½ teaspoon red-pepper flakes

1 small red bell pepper, sliced into strips

1 medium yellow onion, thinly sliced

¼ cup dry white wine, such as Sauvignon Blanc or Pinot Grigio

1 can (14.5 ounces) diced tomatoes

Crusty bread, for serving

Season chicken with salt and pepper. In a 6-quart pressure cooker, heat 1 tablespoon oil over medium-high. Working in batches, add chicken, skin-side down, and cook until browned, about 5 minutes; transfer to a plate.

Heat remaining tablespoon oil over medium. Add mushrooms and cook until browned, about 4 minutes. Add garlic, rosemary, and red-pepper flakes; cook until fragrant, about 1 minute. Add bell pepper and onion; stir to combine. Stir in wine, and cook until reduced by half, about 2 minutes. Stir in tomatoes and chicken, along with any accumulated juices.

Secure lid. Bring to high pressure over medium-high; reduce heat to maintain pressure and cook until chicken is cooked through, 10 minutes. Remove from heat, vent pressure, then remove lid. Season with salt and black pepper and serve.

Kale and White Bean Soup

ACTIVE TIME 25 MINUTES · TOTAL TIME 1 HOUR, PLUS SOAKING

Cannellini beans are a staple of Tuscany's rustic cuisine. Accordingly, we paired them with Tuscan kale. Soaking the beans overnight helps them cook evenly for the creamiest results. SERVES 6 TO 8

- 1 pound dried cannellini beans
- 2 tablespoons olive oil
- 1 small yellow onion, finely chopped
- 2 garlic cloves, minced
- ½ teaspoon red-pepper flakes
- 6 cups chicken or vegetable broth
- 1 large Parmigiano-Reggiano cheese rind (about 2 ounces), plus grated, for serving

- 2 cups water
- 1 bunch Tuscan kale (also called lacinato kale), tough stems and ribs removed, leaves sliced
- 2 teaspoons finely grated lemon zest, plus 2 tablespoons fresh lemon juice

  Coarse salt and freshly ground black pepper

In a 6-quart pressure cooker, cover beans by 2 inches water, bring to a boil, and remove from heat. Let soak, refrigerated, overnight; drain.

Add oil to the pressure cooker, and heat over medium. Add onion, garlic, and red-pepper flakes; cook until onion is translucent, about 4 minutes. Add beans, broth, rind, and the water.

Secure lid. Bring to high pressure over medium-high; reduce heat to maintain pressure and cook until beans are tender, 15 to 20 minutes. Remove from heat, vent pressure, then remove lid. Stir in kale and lemon zest and juice; season with salt and black pepper; and cook over medium heat until kale is tender, 2 minutes. Remove rind before serving. Serve topped with grated cheese.

SECRET INGREDIENT
Never throw out the rind from a wedge
of Parmigiano-Reggiano cheese—it adds lots
of flavor and thickens the texture of soups
and stews like this one. Freeze rinds until you
need them, then just add one to the pot and
let it simmer with the rest of the ingredients.

Beef, Barley, and Vegetable Stew

ACTIVE TIME 20 MINUTES · TOTAL TIME 1 HOUR 10 MINUTES

Butternut squash is a nice switch from carrots in beef stew, and barley brings an unexpected—and wholly welcome—texture and earthiness to the dish. SERVES 6

- 1 pound beef chuck, cut into 3 pieces
  Coarse salt and freshly ground pepper
- 2 tablespoons olive oil
- 3 garlic cloves, minced
- 4 thyme sprigs
- ½ pound new potatoes, scrubbed and halved

- ½ medium butternut squash (1 pound), peeled, seeded, and cut into ½-inch pieces
- ½ cup pearl barley
- 4 cups low-sodium chicken or beef broth
- 2 cups water

Season beef with salt and pepper. In a 6-quart pressure cooker, heat oil over medium-high. Add beef and cook until browned on all sides, about 6 minutes. Add garlic and thyme; cook until fragrant, 1 minute. Add potatoes, squash, barley, broth, and the water.

Secure lid. Bring to high pressure over medium-high heat; reduce heat to maintain pressure and cook until beef is tender, about 45 minutes. Remove from heat, vent pressure, then remove lid. Using two forks, shred beef. Skim fat. Season with salt and pepper.

One Pot, Four Ways
Risotto

ACTIVE TIME 15 MINUTES · TOTAL TIME 35 MINUTES

Rich, creamy risotto in 35 minutes—without all the stirring? Sign us up! These recipes alone should earn the pressure cooker a permanent home in your kitchen. SERVES 4

Risotto with Asparagus and Peas

- 4 tablespoons unsalted butter
- 1 small yellow onion, finely chopped
- 1½ cups Arborio or Carnaroli rice
- 2 tablespoons white wine, such as Sauvignon Blanc or Pinot Grigio
- 4½ cups low-sodium chicken broth
  Coarse salt and freshly ground pepper
- ½ pound asparagus, trimmed and cut into 1-inch pieces
- 1 cup frozen peas, thawed
- ¾ cup grated Parmigiano-Reggiano cheese (3 ounces), plus more for serving
- 1 teaspoon finely grated lemon zest

1. In a 6-quart pressure cooker, melt 2 tablespoons butter over medium. Add onion and sauté until soft, about 4 minutes. Add rice and cook, stirring, 1 minute. Add wine and cook until just evaporated, 30 seconds. Add 3 cups broth; season with salt and pepper.

2. Secure lid. Bring to high pressure over medium-high heat; reduce heat to maintain pressure and cook until rice is tender, 9 minutes. Remove from heat, vent pressure, then remove lid. Stir in remaining 1½ cups broth and the asparagus; cook over medium until tender, 8 minutes. Stir in peas, Parmigiano-Reggiano, lemon zest, and remaining 2 tablespoons butter. Serve immediately, topped with additional cheese.

with Shrimp and Herbs

• In step 1, add 2 minced **garlic** cloves with onion and sauté.

• In step 2, omit asparagus, peas, and lemon zest. Stir in 1 pound peeled, deveined large **shrimp** with remaining 1½ cups broth, and cook on medium until opaque, 3 to 5 minutes. Finish with ¼ cup chopped mixed **fresh herbs,** such as **tarragon** and flat-leaf **parsley.**

with Mushrooms and Thyme

• In step 1, add ½ pound **cremini mushrooms,** trimmed and sliced, and 1 teaspoon fresh **thyme** leaves with onion and sauté.

• In step 2, omit asparagus, peas, and lemon zest.

with Brussels Sprouts and Pancetta

• In step 1, add 4 ounces **pancetta,** finely chopped, and ½ pound **brussels sprouts,** thinly sliced, with onion and sauté.

• In step 2, omit asparagus, peas, and lemon zest.

RISOTTO with
Asparagus and Peas
PAGE 180

RISOTTO
with Shrimp
and Herbs
PAGE 181

RISOTTO
with Mushrooms
and Thyme
PAGE 181

RISOTTO
with Brussels
Sprouts and Pancetta
PAGE 181

Easy Chickpea Curry

ACTIVE TIME 15 MINUTES · TOTAL TIME 40 MINUTES, PLUS SOAKING

Chickpeas, spinach, and potatoes—all common in Indian cooking—stand up to complex spices. If you like heat, serve sliced fresh serrano or jalapeño chiles with the other toppings. SERVES 4

- 8 ounces dried chickpeas
- ¼ cup vegetable oil
- 1 medium onion, thinly sliced
- ¼ cup minced peeled fresh ginger
- 4 garlic cloves, minced
- 2 tablespoons tomato paste
- 1½ teaspoons ground cumin

- 1 teaspoon ground coriander
- 1 pound new potatoes, scrubbed and halved
- 3¼ cups water
- Coarse salt
- 5 ounces baby spinach (5 cups)
- Naan or other flatbread, lime wedges, plain yogurt, and fresh cilantro, for serving

In a 6-quart pressure cooker, cover chickpeas by 2 inches with water, bring to a boil, and remove from heat. Let soak, refrigerated, overnight; drain.

Add oil to pressure cooker, and heat over medium. Add onion, ginger, and garlic; cook until onion begins to soften, 4 minutes. Add tomato paste, cumin, and coriander; cook until fragrant, about 30 seconds. Add chickpeas, potatoes, and the water. Season with salt.

Secure lid. Bring to high pressure over medium-high; reduce heat to maintain pressure and cook until chickpeas are tender, about 20 minutes. Remove from heat, vent pressure, then remove lid. Stir in spinach. Serve with naan, lime wedges, yogurt, and cilantro.

  PRESSURE COOKER

Irish Beef Stew with Stout

ACTIVE TIME 25 MINUTES · TOTAL TIME 45 MINUTES

Irish stout is dark and toasty. The alcohol (and beer flavor) cooks away, so if you are not a stout drinker, don't let that stop you from trying this recipe. If you are, pour a pint with dinner! SERVES 6

- 2 pounds beef chuck, cut into 1½-inch cubes

  Coarse salt and freshly ground pepper
- 2 tablespoons vegetable oil
- 1 medium yellow onion, cut into 1-inch pieces
- 5 garlic cloves, thinly sliced

- 2 tablespoons all-purpose flour
- 1 can (6 ounces) tomato paste
- 1½ pounds new potatoes, scrubbed
- 1 can (14.5 ounces) reduced-sodium beef broth
- 1 cup Irish stout, such as Guinness
- 1 box (10 ounces) frozen peas, thawed

Season beef with salt and pepper. In a 6-quart pressure cooker, heat 1 tablespoon oil over medium-high. Working in batches, add beef and cook until browned on all sides, 6 to 8 minutes, adding more oil as needed.

Add onion and garlic; cook until translucent, about 3 minutes. Stir in flour, and cook 30 seconds. Add tomato paste and cook, stirring, 1 minute. Add potatoes, broth, and stout; season with salt and pepper.

Secure lid. Bring to high pressure over medium-high; reduce heat to maintain pressure and cook until beef is tender, about 20 minutes. Remove from heat, vent pressure, then remove lid. Add peas and heat through.

Pork and Hominy Stew

ACTIVE TIME 25 MINUTES · TOTAL TIME 1 HOUR 10 MINUTES

Warm up with a bowl of posole. The Mexican stew is made better by a variety of toppings. In addition to the avocado and lime shown here, sliced radishes, cilantro, and crumbled tortilla chips are other highly recommended finishing touches. SERVES 6

1¼ pounds boneless pork shoulder, trimmed and cut into 4-inch pieces

Coarse salt and freshly ground pepper

2 tablespoons vegetable oil

1 medium white onion, chopped

4 garlic cloves, minced

2 tablespoons chili powder

4 cups low-sodium chicken broth

2 cups water

2 cans (15 ounces) hominy, drained and rinsed

Chopped avocado and lime wedges, for serving

Season pork with salt. In a 6-quart pressure cooker, heat oil over medium-high. Add pork and cook until browned on all sides, about 8 minutes; transfer to a plate.

Add onion, garlic, and chili powder; sauté until soft, 4 minutes. Add broth and the water; cook, stirring and scraping up browned bits with a wooden spoon. Return pork to pressure cooker.

Secure lid. Bring to high pressure over medium-high heat; reduce heat to maintain pressure and cook until meat is tender, about 45 minutes. Remove from heat, vent pressure, then remove lid. Skim fat. Using two forks, shred pork; then stir in hominy and heat through. Season with salt and pepper. Serve with avocado and lime.

RIPENING AVOCADOS
When they're ready to eat, avocados feel soft—not mushy—if pressed. To speed up the ripening, put firm avocados in a paper bag for a couple of days.

MAXIMIZE THE MUSHROOMS
We tweaked this recipe to include dried porcini mushrooms and their soaking liquid; they add wonderful mushroom flavor. They might seem pricey, but a little goes a long way, and any extras will keep well in the pantry for months.

Beef Stroganoff

ACTIVE TIME 30 MINUTES · TOTAL TIME 1 HOUR 10 MINUTES

There's a reason this rich dish is still a family favorite after all these years: It's just plain delicious. Cooking everything—even the egg noodles—in the pressure cooker is a smart update. SERVES 4 TO 6

---

1 ounce dried porcini mushrooms

1½ cups boiling water

2 pounds boneless short ribs, cut into 2-inch pieces

Coarse salt and freshly ground pepper

2 tablespoons olive oil

1 pound button mushrooms, trimmed and quartered

1 medium onion, thinly sliced

2 cups low-sodium chicken broth

6 ounces egg noodles

⅓ cup sour cream

1 tablespoon plus 1 teaspoon Dijon mustard

½ cup roughly chopped fresh dill, for serving

Soak porcini mushrooms in the boiling water for 10 minutes. Chop mushrooms; strain and reserve mushroom liquid.

Season meat with salt and pepper. In a 6-quart pressure cooker, heat 1 tablespoon oil over medium-high. Working in batches, add meat and cook until browned on all sides, 5 minutes, adding more oil as needed. Transfer to a plate.

Add remaining tablespoon oil, the button mushrooms, and onion; cook, stirring occasionally, until mushrooms are browned, about 6 minutes. Add porcini mushrooms, mushroom liquid, and chicken broth. Return meat to pressure cooker, along with any accumulated juices.

Secure lid. Bring to high pressure over medium-high; reduce heat to maintain pressure and cook until meat is tender, 30 minutes. Remove from heat, vent pressure, then remove lid. Stir in egg noodles and cook, stirring occasionally, over medium until tender, about 7 minutes. Remove from heat. Shred meat and stir in sour cream and mustard. Season with salt and pepper. Serve topped with dill.

Stockpot & Saucepan

Soup's on! Simmer up a pot filled with favorite ingredients. Or will it be pasta tonight? You may not think of that as a one-pot meal, but our streamlined recipes make it possible—and impossibly simple.

The Basics

These pots are both used for boiling and simmering. The primary difference between them is size. Stockpots generally range from six to twenty quarts. They're great for making big batches of soup or stew, or for boiling corn on the cob, lobster, or a lot of pasta. Most have two looped side handles and a tight-fitting lid.

Saucepans usually come in sizes ranging from one to four quarts. A large saucepan (three or four quarts) is a must-have. Use it for medium-size batches of soup and pasta (not to mention making rice and sauces, blanching vegetables, and many other common kitchen jobs). It has one long handle and a tight-fitting lid.

Cooking Tips

- Most soups can be made a couple of days in advance. If you'll be storing freshly made soup, cool it down before refrigerating it by putting the pot in an ice bath. Or transfer the soup to several smaller containers to refrigerate.

- If storing soup that calls for adding delicate greens or fresh herbs at the end of the cooking time, wait to add them until just before serving the soup.

- For one-pot pastas—with ingredients cooked along with the pasta—make sure to time things carefully so everything is done at once. It you use a different type of pasta than we call for in a recipe, check the cooking time on the box and adjust accordingly.

- When you are bringing water to a boil for pasta, always cover it! Leaving it uncovered wastes time and energy.

STOCKPOT

For everyday cooking, eight quarts is
a versatile size. Look for heavy-duty pans
that conduct heat well and won't have
hot spots. A twelve- to fourteen-quart
stockpot is useful for really big batches.
(A very large stockpot is one piece of
cookware that doesn't necessarily have
to be thick and heavy; it is almost always
used for liquids, which don't scorch,
and a very heavy pot would be hard to
handle when full.) Whatever the size,
look for riveted handles that are easy
to hold. A tall, narrow pot can be hard
to see into; opt for one that's wider.

SAUCEPAN

A three- or four-quart pan is indispensable. It's worth investing in heavy-duty
saucepans that conduct heat well and
won't have hot spots. Look for a riveted
handle that feels comfortable and stays
cool even when the pan is hot.

Minestrone

ACTIVE TIME 30 MINUTES · TOTAL TIME 1 HOUR

Minestra is "soup" in Italian, and *minestrone* means "big soup." Packed with vegetables and cannellini beans, our version more than lives up to its name. SERVES 6

- 2 tablespoons olive oil, plus more for serving (optional)
- 1 medium red onion, chopped
- 2 medium carrots, chopped
- 1 large celery stalk, chopped
- ¼ teaspoon red-pepper flakes
- 1 teaspoon minced fresh rosemary, or ¼ teaspoon dried

  Coarse salt and freshly ground black pepper
- 1 can (14.5 ounces) whole peeled tomatoes, drained and finely chopped

- 1 large potato, peeled and chopped
- ¼ head Savoy or green cabbage (½ pound), cored and thinly sliced
- 1 can (15 ounces) cannellini beans, rinsed and drained
- 7 cups low-sodium chicken broth or water
- ½ pound green beans, trimmed and cut into 1-inch pieces
- 1 garlic clove, minced (optional)
- ¼ cup thinly sliced fresh basil, plus small leaves for garnish

  Parmigiano-Reggiano, for serving

In a stockpot, heat oil over medium. Add onion, carrots, celery, red-pepper flakes, rosemary, 1 teaspoon salt, and ¼ teaspoon black pepper. Cook, stirring occasionally, until onion begins to turn golden, 5 to 8 minutes.

Add tomatoes; cook until some of the liquid evaporates, about 1 minute. Add potato, cabbage, cannellini beans, and broth; bring to a boil. Stir in green beans.

Reduce to a simmer, and cook until all the vegetables are tender, about 20 minutes. Season with salt and pepper; stir in garlic, if using, and basil. Serve sprinkled with Parmigiano-Reggiano, and garnish with basil. Drizzle with more oil, if desired.

VARY THE VEGETABLES
Feel free to improvise with ingredients. You might substitute zucchini for green beans, chard for cabbage, or chickpeas for cannellini beans.

Warm Quinoa and Chicken Salad

ACTIVE TIME 15 MINUTES · TOTAL TIME 45 MINUTES

Quick-cooking quinoa is a nutritional powerhouse, packed with protein, iron, and fiber. It is also the foundation for a main-course salad with chicken and springy vegetables. SERVES 4

- 3 tablespoons olive oil, plus more for serving
- 4 scallions, white and green parts separated and thinly sliced lengthwise
- 1 cup quinoa, rinsed and drained
- 1 boneless, skinless chicken breast, halved
- 1 teaspoon finely grated lemon zest, plus 1 tablespoon fresh lemon juice

- 1⅓ cups water
- 1 pound asparagus, trimmed and cut into 1-inch pieces
- ½ cup fresh or frozen peas
- 2 tablespoons chopped fresh flat-leaf parsley leaves
- Coarse salt and freshly ground pepper

In a medium saucepan, heat oil over medium-high. Add scallion whites; cook, stirring constantly, until softened, about 3 minutes. Add quinoa, chicken, lemon zest, and the water; bring to a boil, reduce to a simmer, cover, and cook 11 minutes. Add asparagus and peas, cover, and cook until liquid is absorbed and vegetables are tender, 4 to 5 minutes more.

Remove from heat, and let stand 10 minutes. Shred chicken and fluff quinoa. Add lemon juice and parsley, and season with salt and pepper. Sprinkle with scallion greens and drizzle with oil.

Mushroom and Lima Bean Stew

ACTIVE TIME 35 MINUTES · TOTAL TIME 1 HOUR 40 MINUTES, PLUS SOAKING

If you're looking for a tasty way to work more vegetables into your routine, you've found it. This stew features good-for-you limas, mushrooms (two types!), squash, and kale. SERVES 6 TO 8

- 1 cup dried lima beans
- 2 tablespoons extra-virgin olive oil, plus more as needed
- 1 large onion, chopped
- 4 garlic cloves, thinly sliced
- 8 ounces shiitake mushrooms, stemmed and thinly sliced
- 8 ounces portobello mushrooms, trimmed and cut into 1-inch pieces
- 2 pounds butternut squash, peeled, seeded, and cut into 1-inch pieces
- 1 bay leaf
- 8 cups low-sodium chicken or vegetable broth
- Coarse salt and freshly ground pepper
- 8 ounces kale (½ bunch), stems removed and leaves thinly sliced

Cover beans with cold water, and let sit overnight; drain.

In a stockpot, heat oil over medium. Add onion and garlic; cook until tender, 6 to 8 minutes, then transfer to a bowl.

Working in batches, add mushrooms and cook until golden brown over medium-high, about 5 minutes, adding more oil as needed; transfer to bowl.

Return mushrooms and onions to pot and add squash, beans, bay leaf, and broth. Season with pepper. Bring to a boil, reduce to a simmer, and cover partially. Cook until beans are just tender, 50 to 60 minutes.

Stir in kale and cook until tender, about 5 minutes more. Remove bay leaf. Season stew with salt before serving.

BUYING SEAFOOD

Freshness is crucial. Whenever possible, buy seafood the day you plan to cook it. Don't hesitate to ask your fishmonger where and when it was caught, or to smell the seafood itself: It may smell briny, but should not smell "fishy." If you press your finger into a fillet, it should not leave a mark; the flesh should bounce back.

Cioppino

ACTIVE TIME 30 MINUTES • TOTAL TIME 45 MINUTES

San Francisco's Italian and Portuguese immigrant fishermen are said to have invented this tomato-based stew; they would use their daily catch. You may not be doing the fishing, but you should use whatever seafood looks best at the market. SERVES 4 TO 6

¼ cup extra-virgin olive oil

1 large onion, coarsely chopped

4 garlic cloves, minced

2½ teaspoons fresh thyme leaves

2 teaspoons dried oregano

½ teaspoon red-pepper flakes

1 dried bay leaf

1 can (28 ounces) whole peeled tomatoes, crushed

1¼ cups dry white wine, such as Pinot Grigio

1¼ cups water

1 cup bottled clam juice

2 pounds shell-on king crab legs or Dungeness crab legs (optional)

24 littleneck clams, scrubbed well

1 pound firm, skinless white fish fillets (such as red snapper, sea bass, or halibut), cut into 1½-inch pieces

Coarse salt and freshly ground black pepper

1¼ pounds large shrimp (about 30), peeled and deveined, tails left on if desired

½ cup finely chopped fresh flat-leaf parsley leaves

In a stockpot, heat oil over medium. Add onion and garlic; cook until onion is translucent, 3 to 4 minutes. Stir in thyme, oregano, red-pepper flakes, and bay leaf. Add tomatoes (with their liquid), white wine, the water, and clam juice; bring to a simmer.

Add crab, if using, and clams; simmer, covered, until crab shells turn bright pink and clam shells open, about 10 minutes. Season fish with salt and black pepper. Add fish and shrimp to stockpot; simmer, covered, until fish is opaque and shrimp are pink, 2 to 3 minutes. Discard bay leaf and any unopened clams.

Remove pot from heat. Stir in parsley, and season with salt and pepper before serving.

Split Pea Soup

ACTIVE TIME 30 MINUTES • TOTAL TIME 1 HOUR 15 MINUTES

Ham hocks lend smoky flavor and substance to the diner classic. If you have a leftover ham bone, you can use that instead. SERVES 10

- 2 tablespoons vegetable oil
- 1 medium onion, finely chopped
- 4 small carrots, finely chopped
- 1 celery stalk, finely chopped
- ½ red bell pepper, finely chopped
- 4 garlic cloves, minced
- 2 pounds dried green split peas, picked over, rinsed, and drained
- 1 tablespoon chopped fresh thyme leaves
- 2 dried bay leaves
- 2 small ham hocks (1¼ pounds total), with several ½-inch slits cut into skin
- 10 cups low-sodium chicken broth
  Coarse salt and freshly ground pepper
  Croutons, for serving (optional)

In a stockpot, heat oil over medium-high. Add onion, carrots, celery, bell pepper, and garlic; cook until onion is translucent, about 10 minutes. Add peas, thyme, and bay leaves; cook 2 minutes. Add ham hocks and broth. Bring to a boil, reduce to a simmer, and cook, partially covered, until peas are falling apart, about 45 minutes.

Remove ham hocks from pot. Discard skin and bones; cut meat into ¼-inch pieces. Discard bay leaves. Lightly mash peas with the back of a wooden spoon. Return ham to soup, and season with salt and pepper. Serve with croutons, if desired.

ABOUT SPLIT PEAS
These pulses—dried seeds of legume plants—are split in half for quicker cooking. Unlike beans, they don't need overnight soaking, but they should be rinsed and picked over: Sort through them to take out any debris that might not have been removed during processing.

Sweet Potato and Sausage Soup

ACTIVE TIME 20 MINUTES · TOTAL TIME 40 MINUTES

This is quick enough for a weeknight but special enough for casual entertaining. Double the recipe, and invite friends over—can you think of a better meal to share on a wintry weekend? SERVES 6

- 1 tablespoon extra-virgin olive oil
- 1 large yellow onion, cut into ¾-inch pieces
- 2 garlic cloves, minced
  Coarse salt and freshly ground pepper
- ¾ pound sweet or hot Italian sausage, casings removed
- 2 sweet potatoes (1 pound total), peeled and cut into ½-inch pieces

- 4 cups low-sodium chicken broth
- 2 cups water
- ¾ cup small pasta shells
- 4 cups coarsely chopped mixed leafy greens, such as kale and Swiss chard
  Freshly grated Parmigiano-Reggiano cheese, for serving

In a stockpot, heat oil over medium-high. Add onion and garlic; cook until onion is translucent, about 6 minutes. Season with salt and pepper. Add sausage and cook, breaking up meat with a wooden spoon, until browned, about 5 minutes.

Add sweet potatoes, broth, and water; bring to a boil. Add pasta and cook 3 minutes less than package directions recommend. Reduce to a simmer, add greens, and cook until pasta is tender and greens are wilted, 4 minutes. Serve with Parmigiano-Reggiano.

Pasta with Lentils and Greens

ACTIVE TIME 15 MINUTES · TOTAL TIME 55 MINUTES

The ingredients here sound like the makings of a delicious French salad: lentils, tomatoes, arugula, and feta cheese. Mix the components with pasta for a substantial meatless dinner. SERVES 4

Coarse salt and freshly ground pepper

¾ cup French green lentils, picked over and rinsed

1 garlic clove

¾ pound orecchiette or other short pasta

2 tablespoons extra-virgin olive oil, plus more for drizzling

1½ pints cherry tomatoes (3 cups), halved

1 package (5 ounces) baby arugula or spinach (4 packed cups)

¾ cup crumbled feta cheese (2 ounces), plus more for serving

Cilantro sprigs, for serving

Bring a stockpot of salted water to a boil. Add lentils and garlic, and simmer, partially covered, until lentils are tender but not completely soft, about 30 minutes. Add pasta and cook until al dente, according to package directions; drain.

In the same pot, heat oil over high. Add tomatoes and 1 teaspoon salt; cook until just beginning to break down, about 2 minutes. Return pasta and lentils to pot, along with arugula and feta. Stir to combine. Season with salt and pepper. Serve sprinkled with feta and cilantro and drizzled with oil.

ABOUT FRENCH LENTILS
Sometimes labeled "lentils du Puy" or "green lentils," these are slightly smaller than more common brown lentils, and they hold their shape better when cooked, making them ideal for recipes like this.

  STOCKPOT & SAUCEPAN

Stovetop Clambake

ACTIVE TIME 10 MINUTES · TOTAL TIME 40 MINUTES

Forget digging a pit in the sand. Just layer all the ingredients for the ultimate summer party in a stockpot right in your own kitchen. The meal will come together in less time than it takes to pack a bag for a day at the beach. SERVES 6

- 1¼ cups dry white wine, such as Pinot Grigio
- ¾ cup water
- 6 garlic cloves
- 2 large shallots, quartered (root ends left intact)
- 1½ pounds small red potatoes, scrubbed
- ½ to ¾ teaspoon red-pepper flakes (optional)

- 6 ears corn, shucked and halved
- 5 dozen clams, such as littleneck, scrubbed
- 2 lemons, quartered
- 1 pound shell-on extra-jumbo shrimp (16 to 20)
- 4 tablespoons unsalted butter
- ½ cup chopped fresh flat-leaf parsley leaves
- 2 tablespoons chopped fresh oregano leaves

In a large stockpot, bring wine and the water to a boil. Add garlic, shallots, potatoes, and red-pepper flakes, if using; cover and cook 8 minutes. Add corn, clams, and lemons; cover and cook until clams have opened, 10 to 12 minutes. Add shrimp in a single layer, cover, turn off heat, and let sit until shrimp are opaque throughout, about 3 minutes.

With tongs or a spider, transfer shellfish and vegetables to a serving platter, setting lemons aside; discard any unopened clams. Strain broth through a sieve into a bowl, and whisk in butter, parsley, and oregano. Scrape flesh from half the lemons into broth, discarding skins. Serve shellfish and vegetables with remaining lemons and broth for dipping.

Pasta with Farm-Stand Vegetables

ACTIVE TIME 15 MINUTES • TOTAL TIME 20 MINUTES

Savor every bit of summer while you can. Pick up some peak produce—tomatoes, corn, zucchini, and basil—and turn it into a chunky sauce for pasta, letting every flavor shine. SERVES 4

Coarse salt and freshly ground pepper

¾ pound gemelli or other short pasta

4 ears of corn, kernels removed (3 cups)

2 medium zucchini, grated on the large holes of a box grater (about 2½ cups)

2 tablespoons extra-virgin olive oil, plus more for serving

2 garlic cloves, minced

1 pint cherry tomatoes, halved

¼ cup freshly grated Parmigiano-Reggiano cheese, plus more for serving

½ cup torn fresh basil, plus more for serving

In a stockpot of boiling salted water, cook pasta 1 minute less than package directions recommend. Add corn and cook 1 minute more. Reserve 1 cup pasta water. Add zucchini, then drain.

In the same pot, heat oil over high. Add garlic and cook until fragrant, about 1 minute. Stir in tomatoes; cook, stirring, until they begin to burst, about 3 minutes. Add ½ cup pasta water, and bring to a boil. Stir in pasta mixture and Parmigiano-Reggiano, adding additional pasta water if dry. Stir in basil, and season with salt and pepper. Serve drizzled with oil, and sprinkled with cheese and basil.

213

One Pot, Four Ways Chicken Soup

ACTIVE TIME 20 MINUTES · TOTAL TIME 1 HOUR

There's nothing more gratifying than a bowl of chicken soup—
except maybe one of the variations. A few new ingredients
change the flavor but not the soulful nature of the classic. SERVES 8

Classic Chicken Soup

- 1 whole chicken (about 4 pounds), cut into 8 pieces
- 4 cups low-sodium chicken broth
- 5 cups water
  Coarse salt and freshly ground pepper
- 2 medium yellow onions, thinly sliced
- 4 garlic cloves, crushed
- 4 medium carrots, sliced ½ inch thick on the diagonal
- 2 celery stalks, sliced ¼ inch thick on the diagonal
- 12 sprigs flat-leaf parsley, plus chopped leaves for serving
- 2 ounces angel-hair pasta

1. In a stockpot, combine chicken, broth, the water, and 1 teaspoon salt. Bring to a boil, skimming off foam from surface with a large spoon. Reduce heat to medium-low, and simmer 5 minutes, skimming frequently. Add onions, garlic, carrots, celery, and parsley. Simmer, partially covered, until chicken is cooked through, about 25 minutes.

2. Remove parsley and chicken, discarding back, neck, and parsley. Let cool, then tear meat into bite-size pieces. Skim fat.

3. Return broth to a boil and add pasta; simmer 5 minutes. Stir in 3 cups chicken (reserve remaining chicken for another use).

4. Season soup with salt and pepper. Garnish with chopped parsley before serving.

  STOCKPOT & SAUCEPAN

Chinese Chicken Soup

- In step 1, replace onions with 1 bunch **scallions,** white parts only. Omit carrots. Replace celery with 6 slices peeled fresh **ginger.** Replace parsley with ½ bunch fresh **cilantro.**

- In step 2, after removing chicken, strain soup.

- In step 3, replace angel-hair pasta with **lo mein noodles;** add 3 heads chopped **baby bok choy** and 8 ounces halved **sugar snap peas.**

- In step 4, add low-sodium **soy sauce,** to taste; season with freshly ground **white pepper.** Replace parsley with chopped **scallions.**

Colombian Chicken Soup

- In step 1, replace celery with 1 chopped large **tomato.** Replace parsley with ½ bunch fresh **cilantro.**

- In step 3, replace pasta with 8 ounces **yucca** (or potato), peeled and cut into 1-inch pieces; simmer 30 minutes.

- In step 4, season with **salt** and **pepper,** and drizzle with fresh **lemon juice,** to taste. Serve with chopped fresh **cilantro leaves** and thinly sliced **serrano peppers.**

Thai Chicken Soup

- In step 1, replace onions with 3 quartered **shallots.** Omit carrots. Replace celery with 6 slices peeled fresh **ginger** and 2 stalks smashed **lemongrass.** Omit parsley.

- In step 2, after removing chicken, strain soup.

- In step 3, replace pasta with 1½ ounces **rice vermicelli.**

- In step 4, add **Asian fish sauce,** such as *nam pla* or *nuoc nam,* and **lime juice,** to taste. Replace parsley with fresh **basil** leaves, a **lime** wedge, and sliced **Thai chiles.**

CLASSIC CHICKEN SOUP
PAGE 214

**CHINESE
CHICKEN SOUP**
PAGE 215

**COLOMBIAN
CHICKEN SOUP**
PAGE 215

THAI CHICKEN SOUP
PAGE 215

Black Bean and Almond Soup

ACTIVE TIME 30 MINUTES · TOTAL TIME 50 MINUTES

With canned beans and chicken broth, you can get this hearty cumin-spiced soup on the table in under an hour. An immersion blender also saves time—and cleanup. SERVES 4

- 2 tablespoons extra-virgin olive oil
- 2 cups finely chopped red onion (from 1 large onion)

  Coarse salt and freshly ground pepper
- 4 garlic cloves, finely chopped
- ½ teaspoon ground cumin
- 2 cans (15.5 ounces each) black beans, drained and rinsed

- 4 cups low-sodium chicken broth
- ½ cup lightly packed fresh cilantro leaves, plus more for serving
- ¼ cup sliced almonds, toasted, plus more for serving

  Sliced avocado, for serving

  Plain Greek yogurt or sour cream, for serving

In a medium saucepan, heat oil over medium. Add 1½ cups onion, and season with salt and pepper; cook, stirring occasionally, until softened and golden, about 8 minutes. Add garlic and cumin; cook, stirring, until fragrant, about 1 minute. Add beans and broth; bring to a boil. Reduce heat and simmer until beans are heated through and creamy, about 10 minutes. Let cool 10 minutes.

Using an immersion blender, blend soup, leaving mixture chunky. Add cilantro and almonds, and pulse until beans are coarsely chopped but not pureed (do not over-process). Season with salt and pepper. Divide soup among 4 bowls, and top, dividing evenly, with remaining ½ cup onion, the cilantro, almonds, avocado, and yogurt.

TOASTING NUTS
Spread nuts in a single layer on a rimmed baking sheet. Toast in a 350°F oven until fragrant and just starting to brown; sliced almonds take five to seven minutes. Shake the pan or stir the nuts to flip them over halfway through for even browning.

  STOCKPOT & SAUCEPAN

Gemelli with Pesto and Potatoes

ACTIVE TIME 25 MINUTES · TOTAL TIME 40 MINUTES

Potatoes and pasta? Yes! Add green beans and pesto for a traditional dish from Liguria, Italy. It's excellent warm but also at room temperature, making it great for a picnic or potluck. SERVES 4

½ pound new potatoes, scrubbed and halved

Coarse salt and freshly ground pepper

8 ounces gemelli or other short pasta

8 ounces green beans, trimmed and halved

½ cup pesto (store-bought or homemade; see note below)

Parmigiano-Reggiano cheese, grated, for serving

In a stockpot, cover potatoes with 2 inches water; bring to a boil. Add 1 tablespoon salt and pasta; return to a boil, and cook 2 minutes.

Add green beans. Return to a boil, and cook pasta according to package directions and until vegetables are tender, about 6 minutes. Drain.

Toss pasta mixture and potatoes with pesto. Season with salt and pepper, and top with Parmigiano-Reggiano. Serve warm or at room temperature.

MAKING PESTO
Store-bought works fine, but homemade is a cinch. In a food processor, chop ½ cup toasted pine nuts or walnuts, 4 cups fresh basil leaves, ½ cup grated Parmigiano-Reggiano, 1 garlic clove, and salt and pepper. With machine running, pour in ½ cup olive oil; process until smooth. (Makes 1¼ cups.)

Kimchi Stew with Chicken and Tofu

ACTIVE TIME 20 MINUTES · TOTAL TIME 45 MINUTES

This ingredient list may sound unusual, but everything comes together in a beautifully balanced dish. The foundation is kimchi, a spicy Korean mix of pickled and fermented vegetables. SERVES 6 TO 8

3¾ cups low-sodium chicken broth

2½ cups water

2 bone-in, skinless chicken thighs

1 tablespoon minced garlic

2 teaspoons minced peeled fresh ginger

1 teaspoon minced anchovy fillets

¼ teaspoon coarse salt

2 jars (16 ounces each) kimchi, drained, ½ cup liquid reserved

1 pound silken tofu

3 scallions, white and light-green parts only, thinly sliced crosswise

In a stockpot, bring broth, the water, chicken, garlic, ginger, anchovies, and salt to a boil over high. Reduce heat and simmer until chicken is cooked through, about 15 minutes. Remove from heat.

Transfer chicken to a plate, reserving broth. Let chicken stand until cool enough to handle. Remove meat from bone, and shred into bite-size pieces.

Add chicken, kimchi, and reserved kimchi liquid to pot of cooking broth, and place over low heat. Gently add spoonfuls of tofu to pan, being careful not to break them. Gently shake pan to submerge tofu. Bring to a very gentle simmer, and cook just until tofu is heated through, 3 to 5 minutes. Serve topped with scallions.

ABOUT FERMENTED FOODS
The term "fermented" may not sound enticing, but this group of tasty foods includes yogurt and sauerkraut as well as kimchi. Fermented foods contain beneficial bacteria called probiotics, thought to aid in digestion and support the immune system.

  STOCKPOT & SAUCEPAN

Chickpea Stew with Pesto

ACTIVE TIME 25 MINUTES · TOTAL TIME 25 MINUTES

This nourishing stew has a secret ingredient: stale bread, which acts as a thickener. The not-so-secret ingredient is basil pesto—swirl it into each serving for vibrant color and flavor. SERVES 4

- 3 tablespoons extra-virgin olive oil
- 1 large sweet onion (such as Vidalia), thinly sliced
- 4 celery stalks, thinly sliced
  Coarse salt and freshly ground pepper
- 5 sprigs oregano
- 3 tablespoons tomato paste

- 6 cups vegetable broth
- 2 cans (15.5 ounces each) chickpeas, rinsed and drained
- 3 thick slices stale rustic bread, crusts removed, torn into small pieces
- ¼ cup basil pesto (store-bought or homemade, see recipe on page 221), for serving

In a medium saucepan, heat oil over medium-high. Add onion and celery; season with salt and pepper. Cook until vegetables are golden, about 10 minutes. Add oregano and tomato paste; cook, stirring, until fragrant, 1 minute.

Stir in broth; bring to a boil, then reduce to a simmer and cook until onion is softened, about 5 minutes. Add chickpeas and bread; simmer until thickened, 6 to 8 minutes. Season with salt and pepper. Divide among 4 bowls, and top, dividing evenly, with pesto.

Corn and Shrimp Chowder

ACTIVE TIME 25 MINUTES · TOTAL TIME 40 MINUTES

Sweet corn, smoky bacon, and tender shrimp, all in a creamy broth—a bowlful of this soup is the ideal meal for late summer, when the corn is plentiful and there's just a hint of a chill in the air. SERVES 4

- 4 slices bacon, cut into ½-inch pieces
- 8 scallions, white and green parts separated and thinly sliced crosswise
- 2 medium baking potatoes, peeled and cut into ½-inch pieces
- 2 tablespoons all-purpose flour
- 3 cups milk
- 1 teaspoon seafood seasoning, such as Old Bay
- ½ teaspoon dried thyme
- 2 cups water
- 6 ears corn, kernels removed
- 1 pound large shrimp, peeled and deveined
  Coarse salt and freshly ground pepper
  Oyster crackers (optional), for serving

In a stockpot, cook bacon over medium-high heat until crisp and browned, 4 to 6 minutes. With a slotted spoon, transfer bacon to paper towels to drain.

Add scallion whites and potatoes to pot; cook, stirring, until scallions are softened, 1 to 3 minutes. Add flour and cook, stirring, 1 minute. Add milk, seafood seasoning, thyme, and the water. Bring to a boil, then reduce to a simmer, and cook, stirring occasionally, until potatoes are tender, 10 to 12 minutes. Add corn, shrimp, and scallion greens. Cook until shrimp are just opaque, 2 to 3 minutes. Season with salt and pepper. Serve immediately topped with bacon and crackers, if desired.

CORN OFF THE COB
Standing the cob in a shallow bowl while you're slicing off the kernels means you can catch any that go flying. Scrape the cob with a spoon to get all the pulp and a bit of milky liquid, which is full of flavor.

  STOCKPOT & SAUCEPAN

Miso Soup with Soba Noodles

ACTIVE TIME 25 MINUTES · TOTAL TIME 25 MINUTES

Miso paste makes a savory broth. White miso—used here—has a milder flavor than darker varieties. Soba noodles and tofu make the delicate soup a complete meal. SERVES 4

- 4 cups low-sodium vegetable or chicken broth
- 3 cups water
- ½ pound soba noodles (Japanese buckwheat)
- 2 carrots, cut into matchsticks
- ⅓ pound spinach, stems removed, cut into 1-inch strips
- 6 ounces firm or extra-firm tofu, drained and cut into large pieces
- 3 tablespoons white miso
- 2 scallions, sliced crosswise into 1-inch-long strips

In a medium saucepan, bring broth and 2 cups water to a boil over high heat. Reduce heat to medium-low, add soba noodles, and cook 3 minutes. Add carrots and cook until carrots are crisp-tender, about 2 minutes.

Add spinach and tofu, and stir to combine. Continue to cook just until spinach is wilted and tofu is heated through, about 30 seconds more.

Meanwhile, place miso in a bowl, and stir in 1 cup very hot water until miso dissolves, about 2 minutes. Add mixture to saucepan, stirring to combine. Do not let soup boil once miso has been added. Serve topped with scallions.

COOKING WITH MISO
Because the flavor and healthful qualities of miso are affected when boiled, add it only at the end of cooking.

Lentil Soup with Cauliflower and Cheese

ACTIVE TIME 15 MINUTES • TOTAL TIME 1 HOUR

If you already love lentil soup, prepare to fall head over heels. The classic gets even better with the addition of cauliflower florets and a layer of golden, gooey cheese on top. SERVES 4

- 2 tablespoons extra-virgin olive oil
- 1 small onion, finely chopped
- 1 celery stalk, finely chopped
- 1 medium carrot, finely chopped
- 3 sprigs thyme, plus more for garnish
  Coarse salt and freshly ground pepper
- 1 cup brown lentils, picked over and rinsed
- 4 cups low-sodium chicken broth
- ½ head cauliflower, cored, trimmed, and cut into small florets
- 1 cup shredded Gruyère or Parmigiano-Reggiano cheese (3 ounces)

In a stockpot, heat oil over medium-high. Add onion, celery, carrot, and thyme. Season with salt and pepper. Cook, stirring occasionally, until vegetables are softened, about 8 minutes. Add lentils and broth; bring to a boil. Reduce heat, cover, and simmer until lentils are tender, about 30 minutes. Stir in cauliflower, increase heat to medium-high, and simmer just until cauliflower is crisp-tender, about 3 minutes. Remove thyme; season with salt and pepper.

Preheat broiler with rack 6 inches from heating element. Divide soup among 4 oven-proof ramekins or soup bowls. Top with cheese, and broil until golden and bubbling, 3 to 4 minutes. Serve topped with thyme.

STOCKPOT & SAUCEPAN

Bean and Tomato Soup with Indian Spices

ACTIVE TIME 20 MINUTES · TOTAL TIME 40 MINUTES

This fragrant soup was inspired by a *rajma,* a kidney-bean curry from Northern India. Toasted spices, fresh chiles, and a generous dose of grated ginger make a complex and alluring dish. SERVES 4 TO 6

- 1 tablespoon safflower oil
- 1½ cups finely chopped onion
- 2 tablespoons minced garlic
- 2 tablespoons finely grated peeled fresh ginger
- 1 or 2 green Thai chiles, jalapeño chiles, or other fresh chiles, finely chopped, plus more, sliced, for serving
- 1 teaspoon ground cumin
- 1 teaspoon ground coriander
- ¼ teaspoon ground cinnamon
- ¼ teaspoon ground turmeric
- 2 cans (15.5 ounces each) kidney or pinto beans, rinsed and drained
- 1 can (15 ounces) diced tomatoes, with their juice
- 1½ cups water
- Coarse salt
- Plain yogurt, cilantro sprigs, and pita chips, for serving

In a medium saucepan, heat oil over medium. Add onion and garlic; cook, stirring occasionally, until onion is softened and golden, about 8 minutes. Add ginger, chopped chiles, cumin, coriander, cinnamon, and turmeric; cook, stirring occasionally, until fragrant, about 2 minutes.

Stir in beans, tomatoes, and the water; season with salt. Bring to a boil, reduce heat, and simmer until thickened slightly, about 10 minutes. Coarsely mash a third of the beans in pot using a potato masher or an immersion blender; stir to blend into soup.

Divide soup among bowls, and top with yogurt, cilantro sprigs, and sliced chiles. Serve with pita chips.

Desserts

With main-course recipes as easy and relaxed as the ones in this book, you could choose to prepare something elaborate to end the meal. But why not turn your attention instead to our fuss-free favorites? None of the desserts require much in the way of time or energy, but all are grand enough for any finale.

Peach Crumble

ACTIVE TIME 15 MINUTES • TOTAL TIME 1 HOUR 20 MINUTES

Combine the words "simple" and "dessert," and it's likely a crumble or a crisp will come immediately to mind. We make these crowd-pleasers all year long, with whatever's in season, but peach is our unanimous favorite. SERVES 8

2 pounds peaches, cut into ½-inch wedges

¾ cup granulated sugar

1 tablespoon plus 1 teaspoon cornstarch

1 tablespoon fresh lemon juice

1 teaspoon coarse salt

6 tablespoons unsalted butter, room temperature

¼ cup light-brown sugar

1 cup all-purpose flour

Preheat oven to 375°F. In an 8-inch square baking dish, combine peaches, granulated sugar, cornstarch, lemon juice, and ½ teaspoon salt.

In a bowl, combine butter and brown sugar with a wooden spoon until creamy. Stir in flour and remaining ½ teaspoon salt. Using your hands, mix until large pieces form. Scatter over filling.

Bake until center is bubbling, 40 to 50 minutes, tenting loosely with foil after 30 minutes. Let cool 20 minutes before serving.

Rustic Apple Tart

ACTIVE TIME 20 MINUTES • TOTAL TIME 1 HOUR

With puff pastry in the freezer and a bowl of apples on the counter, there's no question what to have for dessert. Roll out the dough, toss fruit on top, and pop it into the oven. The only hard part is waiting for it to bake and cool. SERVES 6

1 sheet frozen puff pastry (from a standard 17.3-ounce package), thawed

All-purpose flour, for work surface

3 Granny Smith apples

⅓ cup sugar

1 large egg yolk

1 tablespoon plus 1 teaspoon water

2 tablespoons unsalted butter

2 tablespoons apple jelly, or apricot jam

Preheat oven to 375°F. On a lightly floured work surface, roll out folded pastry sheet to an 8-by-14-inch rectangle. Trim edges with a sharp knife. Transfer to a baking sheet; chill in freezer. Peel, core, and slice apples ¼ inch thick; toss with sugar.

Beat egg yolk; then whisk in the teaspoon of water. Brush pastry with egg wash. Use a sharp paring knife to score a ¾-inch border around pastry (do not cut all the way through). Arrange apples inside border, and dot with butter. Bake until pastry is golden and apples are tender, 30 to 35 minutes.

Heat jelly with the tablespoon of water until melted. Brush apples with glaze. Let cool 15 minutes. Serve tart warm or at room temperature.

Skillet Chocolate-Chip Cookie

ACTIVE TIME 10 MINUTES • TOTAL TIME 30 MINUTES

Everyone loves homemade chocolate chip cookies. This brilliant recipe goes one better for the baker—no need to portion out the dough or wait for baking sheets to cool between batches. SERVES 8

- 6 tablespoons unsalted butter, room temperature
- ⅓ cup packed dark-brown sugar
- ½ cup granulated sugar
- 1 large egg
- 1 teaspoon pure vanilla extract
- 1 cup all-purpose flour
- ½ teaspoon baking soda
- ½ teaspoon coarse salt
- 1 cup semisweet chocolate chips

Preheat oven to 350°F. In a bowl, combine butter and both sugars with a wooden spoon until creamy. Stir in egg and vanilla. Stir in flour, baking soda, and salt. Stir in chocolate chips. Transfer to a 10-inch ovenproof skillet (preferably cast iron); smooth top.

Bake until cookie is golden brown and set in the center, 18 to 20 minutes. Let cool 5 minutes before slicing and serving.

Giant Almond Crumble Cookie

ACTIVE TIME 15 MINUTES • TOTAL TIME 50 MINUTES

What's more fun than baking one big cookie? Serving one, right in the middle of the table, and encouraging everybody to break off a piece (or two). This crumbly, nutty treat is known as *torta sbrisolona* in Italy. SERVES 8

- 14 tablespoons (1¾ sticks) unsalted butter, room temperature, plus more for pan
- 1¾ cups all-purpose flour
- 1½ cups (about 5 ounces) blanched almonds, finely ground
- ¾ cup sugar
- ¼ teaspoon coarse salt
- 1½ teaspoons pure vanilla extract

Preheat oven to 350°F. Butter a 10-inch springform pan. In a bowl, whisk together flour, ground almonds, sugar, salt, and vanilla. Cut in the butter with a pastry blender until completely incorporated. Squeeze the mixture together to form pea-size to 1-inch clumps.

Gently press three quarters of the mixture evenly into the prepared pan, and sprinkle evenly with remaining crumbs. Bake until cookie begins to turn golden, about 25 minutes. Reduce oven temperature to 300°F; continue to bake until golden brown, about 10 minutes more. Let cool 5 minutes before serving.

Raspberry Sorbet

ACTIVE TIME 10 MINUTES • TOTAL TIME 40 MINUTES

Three ingredients—frozen raspberries, sugar, and water—never tasted so good. And for this incredibly easy, icy (and even fat-free!) dessert, the food processor does most of the work. SERVES 8

½ cup sugar

½ cup water

2 bags (12 ounces each) frozen raspberries

Stir together sugar and the water until sugar dissolves. Pulse raspberries in a food processor until coarsely chopped. With machine running, pour in sugar-water; pulse until mixture is smooth. Transfer to a 4½-by-8½-inch loaf pan. Cover with plastic, and freeze until firm, about 30 minutes. (The sorbet can be frozen in an airtight container for up to 2 weeks.)

No-Churn Coffee Chocolate-Chip Ice Cream

ACTIVE TIME 10 MINUTES • TOTAL TIME 10 MINUTES, PLUS FREEZING

Homemade ice cream without a machine? Hard to believe, but it's true. The secret ingredient is sweetened condensed milk; the resulting texture is out of this world. Make it the day before you plan to serve it, if possible. SERVES 12

1 tablespoon pure vanilla extract

2 tablespoons instant espresso powder

¾ cup sweetened condensed milk

Coarse salt

2 cups heavy cream

3 ounces bittersweet chocolate, chopped

In a large bowl, combine vanilla and espresso powder; stir until powder has dissolved. Stir in condensed milk and ¼ teaspoon salt.

With an electric mixer on high, beat cream until stiff peaks form, 3 minutes. With a rubber spatula, gently fold whipped cream into condensed milk mixture. Fold in chocolate. Transfer to a 4½-by-8½-inch loaf pan. Cover tightly with plastic wrap, and freeze until firm, at least 12 hours. Let ice cream stand at room temperature 10 minutes before serving. (The ice cream can be frozen in an airtight container for up to 2 weeks.)

Blender Chocolate Mousse

ACTIVE TIME 20 MINUTES • TOTAL TIME 20 MINUTES, PLUS CHILLING

Break out the blender, and bring on the spoons! Our swoon-worthy mousse comes together with a press of a button. Top with whipped cream, chopped nuts, crushed peppermints (for the holidays), or whatever you fancy. SERVES 4

1¼ cups semisweet chocolate chips

3 tablespoons sugar

Pinch of fine salt

⅔ cup whole milk

3 large egg whites

½ cup heavy cream

In a blender, combine chocolate chips, sugar, and salt. In a saucepan, bring milk to a simmer; then transfer to blender. Let stand 1 minute. Blend on high until smooth, 1 minute. Add egg whites and blend on high until well combined, 1 minute. Divide evenly among four 6-ounce dessert cups. Refrigerate until set, 6 hours or up to overnight.

Just before serving, beat cream until soft peaks form. Top each cup with a dollop of whipped cream.

Molten Chocolate Cupcakes

ACTIVE TIME 10 MINUTES • TOTAL TIME 35 MINUTES

We love cupcakes, but not always the time it takes to bake and frost a whole batch. These are in the oven for just 10 minutes and are served warm, with a dusting of confectioner's sugar. What's not to love about that? SERVES 8

6 tablespoons unsalted butter, room temperature

½ cup granulated sugar

4 large eggs

½ cup all-purpose flour

Pinch of coarse salt

11 ounces semisweet chocolate, melted

Confectioners' sugar, for serving

Preheat oven to 400°F. Line a standard muffin tin with paper liners. With an electric mixer on medium-high, beat butter and sugar until light and fluffy, about 2 minutes. Add eggs, one at a time, beating well after each addition. With mixer on low, beat in flour and salt. Beat in chocolate until just combined.

Divide batter evenly among lined cups, filling each about two-thirds full. Bake until tops are just set and no longer shiny, 10 to 11 minutes. Transfer pan to a wire rack to cool, 10 minutes. Remove cupcakes from pans, dust with confectioners' sugar, and serve.

Baked Blackberry Custard

ACTIVE TIME 10 MINUTES · TOTAL TIME 35 MINUTES

Here's our take on clafouti, a French dessert that only sounds fancy. Mix the custard in a blender, pour it over fruit, and bake. It's sure to become one of your specialties, with whatever fruit's in season. SERVES 6

- ¾ cup whole milk
- 3 large eggs
- ½ cup plus 1 tablespoon sugar
- ½ cup all-purpose flour
- ¼ teaspoon coarse salt
- ½ teaspoon pure vanilla extract
- 4 tablespoons unsalted butter, melted
- 2 cups blackberries

Preheat oven to 400°F. In a blender, combine milk, eggs, ½ cup sugar, the flour, salt, and vanilla. Add melted butter; blend mixture until smooth, 30 seconds. Spread berries in a single layer in a pie plate or baking dish, and pour batter over top. Sprinkle with remaining tablespoon sugar, and bake until slightly puffed and just set in middle, 20 to 25 minutes. Serve warm.

Fruit Skillet Cake

ACTIVE TIME 15 MINUTES · TOTAL TIME 1 HOUR

This versatile batter takes kindly to stone fruits like plums (shown here), peaches, and even cherries. Try it in fall with apples or pears, in spring with berries—you get the idea. SERVES 6

- 4 tablespoons unsalted butter, room temperature, plus more for skillet
- 1 cup all-purpose flour, plus more for skillet
- ½ teaspoon baking powder
- ¼ teaspoon baking soda
- ½ teaspoon coarse salt
- ¾ cup plus 2 tablespoons sugar
- 1 large egg
- ½ cup buttermilk
- 2 ripe medium plums, thinly sliced

Preheat oven to 375°F. Butter an 8-inch ovenproof skillet (preferably cast iron), and dust with flour. Whisk together flour, baking powder, baking soda, and salt. With an electric mixer on medium, beat butter and ¾ cup sugar until pale and fluffy, 3 to 5 minutes. Beat in egg. Add flour mixture in 3 batches, alternating with buttermilk; beat until combined.

Transfer batter to the prepared skillet; smooth top. Arrange plums on top, fanning the slices; sprinkle with the remaining 2 tablespoons sugar.

Bake until golden brown and a cake tester into center comes out clean, 35 to 40 minutes. Transfer to a wire rack to cool slightly before serving.

Acknowledgments

This book represents the creativity of many individuals who are not only talented recipe developers, editors, and art directors, but also passionate home cooks themselves. Thank you to editor at large Sarah Carey for overseeing the content creation of this book, and to the rest of Martha Stewart Living Omnimedia's food team, past and present, led by Lucinda Scala Quinn and Jennifer Aaronson.

Thank you to editorial director Ellen Morrissey for her ideas and leadership, and to editors Amy Conway, Evelyn Battaglia, and Susanne Ruppert for curating a collection of excellent recipes and turning them into this indispensable book. Deputy art director Gillian MacLeod, with the guidance of design director Jennifer Wagner, created a design for the book that is as simple and elegant as the recipes within, as well as the charming illustrations throughout. Samantha Seneviratne and Jessie Damuck brought their culinary talents to the project. Elizabeth Eakin and John Myers provided considerable assistance in producing the pages, along with Denise Clappi, Alison Vanek Devine, Kiyomi Marsh, and Ryan Monaghan. Katie Holdefehr cheerfully supported the team along the way. As always, chief content director Eric A. Pike's input was invaluable. Thank you as well to Meg Lappe, Josefa Palacio, Gertrude Porter, Kirsten Rodgers, and Erin Rouse.

Photographer Christina Holmes did a beautiful job of producing the bulk of the new images. A complete list of contributing photographers appears opposite. Prop stylists Megan Hedgpeth and Pam Morris and art director James Dunlinson brought their finely honed sensibilities to the pages as well.

Our colleagues in Martha Stewart Living Omnimedia's merchandising department provided the beautiful Martha Stewart Collection for Macy's pots, pans, and other kitchenware seen in many of the photographs.

We are proud to work hand-in-hand with our longtime partners at Clarkson Potter, especially publisher Pam Krauss, associate publisher Doris Cooper, creative director Marysarah Quinn, art director Jane Treuhaft, production director Linnea Knollmueller, production editorial director Mark McCauslin, and associate editor Jessica Freeman-Slade. And special thanks to our former editors, Emily Takoudes and Angelin Borsics, for their help along the way.

Photo Credits

Sang An: page 20

William Brinson: pages 117, 121

Christina Holmes: pages 2-11, 13, 15, 19, 26-27, 37, 38, 45, 52-53, 55, 69, 72-73, 89, 98-99, 101, 103, 104, 111, 114-115, 118, 124-125, 127, 129, 141, 144-147, 149, 153, 157, 161, 168-169, 171, 174, 177, 178, 182-183, 185, 186, 190, 192-193, 195, 197, 198, 201, 202, 205, 209, 213, 216-217, 228, 234-235, 237, 238, 241, 242, 245, 248

John Kernick: pages 30, 94, 133

Yunhee Kim: page 108

Ryan Liebe: pages 154, 162

Jonathan Lovekin: pages 76, 166

Gillian MacLeod: illustrations on pages 25, 71, 113, 143, 181, 215, running feet

David Malosh: pages 42, 90, 130, 219, 231

Johnny Miller: pages 23, 29, 34, 46, 65, 83, 86-87, 97, 107, 122, 138, 150, 165, 223

Marcus Nilsson: pages 41, 58, 134

Con Poulos: pages 33, 61, 206, 210

David Prince: page 57

Andrew Purcell: pages 49, 66, 75, 79, 93, 137, 158, 173, 189, 220, 224, 227

Hector Sanchez: page 62

Anna Williams: page 232

Romulo Yanes: pages 16, 50, 80

Index